Capitalism

Opposing Viewpoints

Bruno Leone

GREENHAVEN PRESS INC.
1611 POLK ST. N.E.
MINNEAPOLIS, MINNESOTA 55413

SERIES EDITORS: DAVID L. BENDER AND GARY E. McCUEN

HB
501
.C3

© Copyright 1978 by Greenhaven Press, Inc.

ISBN 0-912616-50-4 Paper Edition

ISBN 0-912616-51-2 Library Edition

99332

Capitalism

Contents

Capitalism

Preface

In its broadest sense, capitalism is an economic principle which probably predates recorded history. As long as a demand has existed for goods and individuals have been available to satisfy that demand at a personal profit, capitalism may be said to have existed. It was not until the 18th and 19th centuries in Europe that modern capitalism was born. It grew out of a series of philosophical, technological, and economic developments which combined to give rise to modern industry and its accompanying market system. (Historians refer to the period as the Industrial Revolution.)

Popularly known as the "free-enterprise system," modern capitalism is distinguished from its economic predecessors by certain features which include: the private and corporate ownership of factories and other production facilities; a system of markets in which individuals and corporations purchase and sell goods and services; a labor force legally free to choose any available avenue of employment; the sale of labor for money; the universal use of money for the purchase of goods; and the growth of technology.

Previously, the absence of machinery restricted the amount of goods produced which, in turn, placed limitations upon the economic system. However, during the Industrial Revolution, the hand labors of artisans and their apprentices, private barter, and other modes of production and economic exchange disappeared or became quaint remnants of days past. In their place, mechanized industries began spreading throughout Western Europe, America, and eventually the entire world. Along with this change, free and competitive markets replaced governmental regulation of national economies.

The new system was met with extreme reactions. It was hailed as a boon by some and condemned as a monster by others. To the good, it was argued that capitalism was creating an abundance of jobs by greatly expanding the productive market. Along

1

with the market, national economies were growing at an unprecedented rate. And finally, both the quantity and quality of goods available for public consumption were experiencing a significant improvement. To the bad, a sympathetic finger was pointed at the unfortunate worker, one of the primary architects of this fabulous new economic structure. Men, women, and children were required to labor excessively long hours, often in unsafe and bestial surroundings, for a bare, subsistence wage. The gap between rich and poor (owner and worker) increased as rapidly as industry grew. However significant were the economic achievements of capitalism, socially, opponents said, it was a depressing moral failure.

The following chapters explore the evolution of this controversy. The readings offer both the theoretical and practical positions for and against capitalism. However, the reader is asked to note that while the arguments continually change to suit contemporary circumstances, their tone remains consistently passionate.

Chapter 1

Capitalism:

Smith and Marx:
The Germinal Arguments

INTRODUCTION

One of the first and most persuasive advocates of modern capitalism was Adam Smith. A Scotsman, Smith became (and still remains) the prophet of the new economic order. In his epochal work, *The Wealth of Nations*, he provided a compelling and all-inclusive rationale for the capitalistic system. It is to his credit that contemporary defenders of the principle parrot his basic arguments virtually unchanged.

The fundamental theme of *The Wealth of Nations* is what Smith's later supporters termed the doctrine of laissez-faire ("hands-off") capitalism. The doctrine held that the world of economics functions under "natural laws" which operate exclusive of politics. Government intervention in the economic order of things will upset these "natural laws" and thereby disrupt a nation's economy. However, by maintaining a "hands-off" policy and allowing private citizens complete economic freedom, governments can ensure the growth of a nation's wealth.

Smith realized that under a free enterprise system, individuals would pursue their own self-interests. Anticipating his critics, Smith contended, however, that self-serving individuals, with the help of an "invisible hand" (i.e., competition), would be contributing to the welfare of all. In other words, in order to build and maintain a flourishing and profitable concern, a businessman's products would have to be needed, well made, and competitively priced. If not, he would be unable to compete successfully with others also pursuing their self-interests. Moreover, he would be creating jobs and helping to expand the general economy. Thus the "natural laws" of economics, when unrestrained, would profit not only industry but government and labor as well.

The most serious challenge to Adam Smith and his followers came from Karl Marx, a 19th century German. The son of a Prussian lawyer, the methodical Marx proved a worthy and resourceful opponent. He unfolded his economic theories in his monumental *Das Kapital* (*Capital*), a work on which he spent eighteen years researching and writing.

Marx's primary objection to the capitalistic system was that it was grossly unfair to the worker. To illustrate this, he developed his now famous theory of "surplus value." The theory involves the intricate relationship between the worker and his product and the employer and his profit. In effect, Marx was saying that the worker received as salary only a small part of the value of the goods produced. The difference between the cost of labor and the price at which a product was sold constituted the employer's profit. Hence, "surplus value" represented that monetary portion of a product for which a worker toiled but received no pay. In brief, the theory implied that whatever profits the capitalist class acquired, it stole from the workers.

Marx's solution to this exploitative situation was a simple one. The means of production and exchange should be taken from the capitalists and turned over to the workers. This would eliminate the problem of "surplus value," since the working class would be producing and exchanging goods for itself as a collective unit.

The following readings are taken from Smith's *The Wealth of Nations* and Marx's *Manifesto of the Communist Party*, co-authored with Frederick Engels. The readings offer some of the essential features of the philosophy of each thinker.

The Wealth
of Nations

Adam Smith

Adam Smith (1723-1790), a political economist, was born in Scotland. He was educated at the universities of Glasgow and Oxford and later taught English Literature, economics, logic, and moral philosophy at Glasgow University. In 1776, Smith published *The Wealth of Nations.* Systematic, comprehensive, and forceful, the work was an immediate success and became widely recognized by businessmen and statesmen as the authoritative statement on political economy. In the following reading, Smith explains why individual ''self-interest'' is beneficial to society as a whole and why governmental intervention in business retards ''the progress of society towards real wealth and greatness.''

Consider the following questions while reading:

1. How does self-interest benefit society?
2. Of what value is the profit motive?
3. How can the government retard progress?

Adam Smith, **The Wealth of Nations** (New York: Random House, 1965), pp. 421-23, 650-51.

THE RELATIONSHIP OF CAPITAL TO EMPLOYMENT

The general industry of the society never can exceed what the capital of the society can employ. As the number of workmen that can be kept in employment by any particular person must bear a certain proportion to his capital, so the number of those that can be continually employed by all the members of a great society, must bear a certain proportion to the whole capital of that society, and never can exceed that proportion. No regulation of commerce can increase the quantity of industry in any society beyond what its capital can maintain. It can only divert a part of it into a direction into which it might not otherwise have gone; and it is by no means certain that this artificial direction is likely to be more advantageous to the society than that into which it would have gone of its own accord.

SELF-INTEREST BENEFITS SOCIETY

Every individual is continually exerting himself to find out the most advantageous employment for whatever capital he can command. It is his own advantage, indeed, and not that of the society, which he has in view. But the study of his own advantage naturally, or rather necessarily leads him to prefer that employment which is most advantageous to the society.

First, every individual endeavours to employ his capital as near home as he can, and consequently as much as he can in the support of domestic industry; provided always that he can thereby obtain the ordinary, or not a great deal less than the ordinary profits....

THE PROFIT MOTIVE

Secondly, every individual who employs his capital in the support of domestic industry, necessarily endeavours so to direct that industry, that its produce may be of the greatest possible value.

The produce of industry is what it adds to the subject or materials upon which it is employed. In proportion as the value of this produce is great or small, so will likewise be the profits of the employer. But it is only for the sake of profit that any man employs a capital in the support of industry; and he will always, therefore, endeavour to employ it in the support of that industry of which the produce is likely to be of the greatest

7

value, or to exchange for the greatest quantity either of money or of other goods.

WHAT IS CAPITAL

Capital is that part of the wealth of a country which is employed in production, and consists of food, clothing, tools, raw materials, machinery, etc., necessary to give effect to labour.

David Ricardo, **Principles of Political Economy and Taxation.**

THE "INVISIBLE HAND" AND SOCIETY

But the annual revenue of every society is always precisely equal to the exchangeable value of the whole annual produce of its industry, or rather is precisely the same thing with that exchangeable value. As every individual, therefore, en-deavours as much as he can both to employ his capital in the support of domestic industry, and so to direct that industry that its produce may be of the greatest value; every individual necessarily labours to render the annual revenue of the society as great as he can. He generally, indeed, neither intends to promote the public interest, nor knows how much he is promot-ing it. By preferring the support of domestic to that of foreign industry, he intends only his own security; and by directing that industry in such a manner as its produce may be of the greatest value, he intends only his own gain, and he is in this, as in many other cases, led by an invisible hand to promote an end which was no part of his intention. Nor is it always the worse for the society that it was no part of it. By pursuing his own interest he frequently promotes that of the society more effectually than when he really intends to promote it. I have never known much good done by those who affected to trade for the public good....

THE SUPERIOR JUDGMENT OF THE CAPITALIST

What is the species of domestic industry which his capital can employ, and of which the produce is likely to be of the greatest value, every individual, it is evident, can, in his local situation, judge much better than any statesman or lawgiver can do for him. The statesman, who should attempt to direct private people in what manner they ought to employ their capitals, would not only load himself with a most unnecessary attention, but assume an authority which could safely be trusted, not only to no single person, but to no council or senate whatever, and which would nowhere be so dangerous as in the hands of a man who had folly and presumption enough to fancy himself fit to exercise it....

GOVERNMENT CAN RETARD PROGRESS

It is thus that every system which endeavours, either, by extraordinary encouragements, to draw towards a particular species of industry a greater share of the capital of the society than what would naturally go to it; or, by extraordinary restraints, to force from a particular species of industry some share of the capital which would otherwise be employed in it; is in reality subversive of the great purpose which it means to promote. It retards, instead of accelerating, the progress of the society towards real wealth and greatness; and diminishes, instead of increasing, the real value of the annual produce of its land and labour....

THE SOLE DUTIES OF GOVERNMENT

Every man, as long as he does not violate the laws of justice, is left perfectly free to pursue his own interest his own way, and to bring both his industry and capital into competition with those of any other man, or order of men. The sovereign* is completely discharged from a duty, in the attempting to perform which he must always be exposed to innumerable delusions, and for the proper performance of which no human wisdom or knowledge could ever be sufficient; the duty of superintending the industry of private people, and of directing it towards the employments most suitable to the interest of the society. According to the system of natural liberty, the sovereign has only three duties to attend to; three duties of great importance, indeed, but plain and intelligible to common understandings: first, the duty of protecting the society from the violence and invasion of other independent societies; secondly, the duty of protecting, as far as possible, every member of the society from the injustice or oppression of every

*Government.

9

other member of it, or the duty of establishing an exact administration of justice; and, thirdly, the duty of erecting and maintaining certain public works and certain public institutions, which it can never be for the interest of any individual, or small number of individuals, to erect and maintain; because the profit could never repay the expence to any individual or small number of individuals, though it may frequently do much more than repay it to a great society.

The Manifesto of the Communist Party

Karl Marx

Karl Marx (1818-1883) is considered to be the father of modern scientific socialism. Educated in Germany at the universities of Bonn, Berlin, and Jena, Marx turned to communism* while in Paris as a result of further studies in philosophy, history, and political science. In 1844, he met Frederick Engels , with whom he collaborated to systematize the theoretical principles of communism. Although his influence was small during his lifetime, it grew enormously with the spread of socialism and the growth of the labor movement. The reading below, an excerpt from *The Manifesto of the Communist Party*, was written by Marx on the basis of a draft prepared by Engels. Some of the fundamental concepts of communism are outlined therein.

Consider the following questions while reading:

1. What are the two great classes?
2. How have the workers been exploited?
3. What is the role of the proletariat?
4. What is the aim of communism?

*For the distinction between socialism and communism, see the volume on communism in the ISMS series.

Karl Marx and Frederick Engels, **Manifesto of the Community Party** (Peking: Foreign Languages Press, 1970), pp. 30-31, 33-34, 38-40, 46-48, 76.

BOURGEOISIE AND PROLETARIAT

The history of all hitherto existing society is the history of class struggles.

Our epoch, the epoch of the bourgeoisie, possesses, however, this distinctive feature: it has simplified the class antagonisms. Society as a whole is more and more splitting up into two great hostile camps, into two great classes directly facing each other: Bourgeoisie and Proletariat*....

The bourgeoisie has, since the establishment of Modern Industry and of the world market, conquered for itself, in the modern representative State, exclusive political sway. The executive of the modern State is but a committee for managing the common affairs of the whole bourgeoisie.

BOURGEOIS EXCESSES

The bourgeoisie, historically, has played a most revolutionary part.

The bourgeoisie, wherever it has got the upper hand, has put an end to all feudal, patriarchal, idyllic relations. It has pitilessly torn asunder the motley feudal ties that bound man to his "natural superiors," and has left remaining no other nexus between man and man than naked self-interest, than callous "cash payment." It has drowned the most heavenly ecstasies of religious fervour, of chivalrous enthusiasm, of philistine sentimentalism, in the icy water of egotistical calculation. It has resolved personal worth into exchange value, and in place of the numberless indefeasible chartered freedoms, has set up that single, unconscionable freedom — Free Trade. In one word, for exploitation, veiled by religious and political illusions, it has substituted naked, shameless, direct, brutal exploitation.

The bourgeoisie has stripped of its halo every occupation hitherto honoured and looked up to with reverent awe. It has converted the physician, the lawyer, the priest, the poet, the man of science, into its paid wage-labourers.

*By bourgeoisie is meant the class of modern Capitalists, owners of the means of social production and employers of wage-labour. By proletariat, the class of modern wage-labourers who, having no means of production of their own, are reduced to selling their labour-power in order to live. [Note by Engels to the English edition of 1888.]

The bourgeoisie has torn away from the family its sentimental veil, and has reduced the family relation to a mere money relation....

The conditions of bourgeois society are too narrow to comprise the wealth created by them. And how does the bourgeoisie get over [this]? On the one hand by enforced destruction of a mass of productive forces; on the other, by the conquest of new markets, and by the more thorough exploitation of the old ones. That is to say, by paving the way for more extensive and more destructive crises, and by diminishing the means whereby crises are prevented.

Karl Marx

CAPITALISM IS SELF-DESTRUCTIVE

Capitalism did not arise because capitalists stole the land or the workmen's tools, but because it was more efficient than feudalism. It will perish because it is not merely less efficient than socialism, but actually self-destructive.

J.B.S. Haldane, I Believe.

The weapons with which the bourgeoisie felled feudalism [its predecessor] to the ground are now turned against the bourgeoisie itself.

But not only has the bourgeoisie forged the weapons that bring death to itself; it has also called into existence the men who are to wield those weapons — the modern working class — the proletarians.

THE ROLE OF THE PROLETARIAT

In proportion as the bourgeoisie, *i.e.*, capital, is developed, in the same proportion is the proletariat, the modern working class, developed — a class of labourers, who live only so long as they find work, and who find work only so long as their labour increases capital. These labourers, who must sell themselves piecemeal, are a commodity, like every other article of commerce, and are consequently exposed to all the vicissitudes of competition, to all the fluctuations of the market.

Owing to the extensive use of machinery and to division of labour, the work of the proletarians has lost all individual character, and, consequently, all charm for the workman. He becomes an appendage of the machine, and it is only the most simple, most monotonous, and most easily acquired knack, that is required of him. Hence, the cost of production of a workman is restricted, almost entirely, to the means of subsistence that he requires for his maintenance, and for the propagation of his race. But the price of a commodity, and therefore also of labour, is equal to its cost of production. In proportion, therefore, as the repulsiveness of the work increases, the wage decreases. Nay more, in proportion as the use of machinery

14

and division of labour increases, in the same proportion the burden of toil also increases, whether by prolongation of the working hours, by increase of the work exacted in a given time or by increased speed of the machinery, etc.

THE EXPLOITATION OF THE WORKER

Modern industry has converted the little workshop of the patriarchal master into the great factory of the industrial capitalist. Masses of labourers, crowded into the factory, are organised like soldiers. As privates of the industrial army they are placed under the command of a perfect hierarchy of officers and sergeants. Not only are they slaves of the bourgeois class, and of the bourgeois State; they are daily and hourly enslaved by the machine, by the overlookers, and, above all, by the individual bourgeois manufacturer himself. The more openly this despotism proclaims gain to be its end and aim, the more petty, the more hateful and the more embittering it is.

The less the skill and exertion of strength implied in manual labour, in other words, the more modern industry becomes developed, the more is the labour of men superseded by that of women. Differences of age and sex have no longer any distinctive social validity for the working class. All are instruments of labour, more or less expensive to use, according to their age and sex.

No sooner is the exploitation of the labourer by the manufacturer, so far, at an end, that he receives his wages in cash, than he is set upon by the other portions of the bourgeoisie, the landlord, the shopkeeper, the pawnbroker, etc....

THE BOURGEOISIE: ITS OWN GRAVE-DIGGER

The essential condition for the existence, and for the sway of the bourgeois class, is the formation and augmentation of capital; the condition for capital is wage-labour. Wage-labour rests exclusively on competition between the labourers. The advance of industry, whose involuntary promoter is the bourgeoisie, replaces the isolation of the labourers, due to competition, by their revolutionary combination, due to association. The development of Modern Industry, therefore, cuts from under its feet the very foundation on which the bourgeoisie produces and appropriates products. What the bourgeoisie, therefore, produces, above all, are its own grave-diggers. Its fall and the victory of the proletariat are equally inevitable....

THE AIM OF COMMUNISM

The immediate aim of the Communists is the same as that of all the other proletarian parties: formation of the proletariat into a class, overthrow of the bourgeois supremacy, conquest of political power by the proletariat....

The Communists disdain to conceal their views and aims. They openly declare that their ends can be attained only by the forcible overthrow of all existing social conditions. Let the ruling classes tremble at a Communistic revolution. The proletarians have nothing to lose but their chains. They have a world to win.

WORKING MEN OF ALL COUNTRIES, UNITE!

Exercise  **1**

Separating Fact From Opinion

FACT AND OPINION

This discussion exercise is designed to promote experimentation with one's ability to distinguish between fact and opinion. It is a fact, for example, that the United States was militarily involved in the Vietnam War. But to say that this involvement served the interests of world peace is an opinion. Future historians will agree that American soldiers fought in Vietnam, but their interpretations about the causes and consequences of the war will probably vary greatly.

Some of the following statements are taken from reading number five and some have other origins. Consider each statement carefully. Mark (O) by any statement which you feel is an opinion or interpretation of the facts. Mark (F) by any statement which you believe is a fact. Then discuss and compare your judgments with those of other class members.

O = OPINION
F = FACT

_____ 1. Americans owe their remarkable material development to our competitive economic system.

_____ 2. Our economic system based on greed is largely responsible for the poverty and crime in our large cities.

_____ 3. It is possible for a nation to have a socialist economy and a democratic political system.

_____ 4. It is not possible for a nation to have a socialist economy and a democratic political system.

_____ 5. Capitalism might not work well in some nations.

_____ 6. Socialism works well in poor nations that have little industrial development.

_____ 7. The U.S. economy is mixed, using both elements of capitalism and socialism.

_____ 8. Most Americans would not favor a socialist economy.

_____ 9. Americans should not interfere with nations that prefer to establish socialist and communist societies.

_____ 10. It is possible to be a socialist and not a communist.

_____ 11. France is a nation with a democratic political system.

_____ 12. Capitalism is based on greed and the pursuit of profit.

_____ 13. Socialism is based on cooperation and a just sharing of the wealth.

_____ 14. Socialism is a more just system of economics than capitalism.

_____ 15. Socialism is too idealistic and will never work.

Chapter **2**

Capitalism:

The Nineteenth Century: Capitalism and Labor

INTRODUCTION

The Industrial Revolution and the accompanying rise of capitalism brought about profound changes in the economic and social order of Western European society. Experiencing little or no governmental interference, the early industries flourished and, as prophesied by Smith, so did the wealth of nations. The success of the new system resulted from the efforts of two highly distinguishable classes, the capitalists who financed the industries and the workers who were employed within them. In the 19th century, however, the capitalists, for the most part, were the system's prime beneficiaries. The nature of early industry was such that the profits enjoyed by the owners were generated by the toil of the hapless workers.*

In the absence of governmental regulation and effective employee organizations, working conditions were usually extremely poor and wages dismally low. The work day averaged twelve to fourteen hours and ran as high as nineteen hours during busy periods. Women and children were employed under conditions similar to men, receiving only half to a quarter of the wages paid men. In most factories, the machinery was propelled by large gear wheels which often had no protective coverings. It was not unusual for a worker to mangle or lose a finger, hand, or arm in one of these machines. There were no benefits such as sick leave and workman's compensation. Indeed, an individual injured on the job was required to meet his or her own medical expenses and suffer a complete salary loss while recuperating. Finally, the living conditions of the worker were as impoverished as the working conditions.

The following readings attempt to illustrate the socio-economic circumstances of 19th century labor. The readings supportive of capitalism defend the system on the basis of natural law, the

*There were noteable exceptions. Foremost among them was Robert Owen (1771-1858), a British industrialist who rose from a laborer in a cotton factory to part-owner of a mill in New Lanark, Scotland. Mindful of his humble origin, Owen took an active interest in the welfare of his workers and converted New Lanark into a model factory town.

merits of ''self-help,'' and the visible improvement it represented over the previous period. The opposing viewpoints look
no further than the worker to underscore their assertion that
radical reform was morally imperative.

**Before the days of child labor laws, women and children work
in a bean processing plant (c. 1900).** United Press International, Inc.

Viewpoint  3

England:
The Worker's Paradise

Andrew Ure

Andrew Ure (1778-1857) was one of England's
staunchest defenders of the factory system.
Born in Scotland, he received his MD from
Edinburgh University in 1801 and went on to
teach chemistry and natural philosophy at
Anderson's College, Glasgow. Ure wrote and
lectured extensively on popular scientific
subjects in an effort to enlighten the common
person of his day. In the following reading from
his *Philosophy of Manufactures*, he takes the
position that the living and working standards
in 19th century England were far better than
those of the pre-industrial age.

Consider the following questions while reading:

1. What are the blessings of the machine age?
2. How are children treated in the factories?
3. What kind of wages are paid in the factories?

Andrew Ure, **The Philosophy of Manufacturers** (London: Frank Cass & Co., 1967), pp. 6-7, 396,
306, 389-90, 290, 299, 301. Reprinted with permission.

ENGLAND AFTER THE MACHINE AGE

This island* is pre-eminent among civilized nations for the prodigious development of its factory wealth, and has been therefore long viewed with a jealous admiration by foreign powers. This very pre-eminence, however, has been contemplated in a very different light by many influential members of our own community, and has been even denounced by them as the certain origin of innumerable evils to the people, and of revolutionary convulsions to the state. If the affairs of the kingdom be wisely administered, I believe such allegations and fears will prove to be groundless, and to proceed more from the envy of one ancient and powerful order of the commonwealth,** towards another suddenly grown into political importance than from the nature of things....***

The blessings which physico-mechanical science has bestowed on society, and the means it has still in store for ameliorating the lot of mankind, have been too little dwelt upon; while, on the other hand, it has been accused of lending itself to the rich capitalists as an instrument for harassing the poor, and of exacting from the operative an accelerated rate of work. It has been said, for example, that the steam-engine now drives the power-looms with such velocity as to urge on their attendant weavers at the same rapid pace; but that the hand-weaver, not being subjected to this restless agent, can throw his shuttle and move his treddles at his convenience. There is, however, this difference in the two cases; that in the factory, every member of the loom is so adjusted that the driving force leaves the attendant nearly nothing at all to do, certainly no muscular fatigue to sustain, while it procures for him good, unfailing wages, besides a healthy workshop *gratis*: whereas the non-factory weaver, having everything to execute by muscular exertion, finds the labor irksome, makes in consequence innumerable short pauses, separately of little account, but great when added together; earns therefore proportionally low wages, while he loses his health by poor diet and the dampness of his hovel. Dr. Carbutt of Manchester says, ''With regard to Sir Robert Peel's assertion a few evenings ago, that the hand-

*England
**Aristocracy
***Bourgeoisie

23

loom weavers are mostly small farmers, nothing can be a greater mistake; they live, or rather they just keep life together, in the most miserable manner, in the cellars and garrets of the town, working sixteen or eighteen hours for the merest pittance.''....

SCIENTIFIC IMPROVEMENT

The constant aim and effect of scientific improvement in manufactures are philanthropic, as they tend to relieve the workmen either from niceties of adjustment which exhaust his mind and fatigue his eyes, or from painful repetition of effort which distort or wear out his frame.

Andrew Ure, **The Philosophy of Manufactures**.

KINDNESS TOWARD CHILDREN

Nothing shows in a clearer point of view the credulity of mankind in general, and of the people of these islands in particular, than the ready faith which was given to the tales of cruelty exercised by proprietors of cotton-mills towards young children....The millowner, in fact, could never interefere but beneficially for the children....

I have visited many factories, both in Manchester and in the surrounding districts, during a period of several months, entering the spinning rooms unexpectedly, and often alone, at different times of the day, and I never saw a single instance of corporal chastisement inflicted on a child, nor indeed did I ever see children in ill-humor. They seemed to be always cheerful and alert, taking pleasure in the light play of their muscles — enjoying the mobility natural to their age. The scene of industry, so far from exciting sad emotions in my mind, was always exhilarating. It was delightful to observe the nimbleness with which they pieced the broken ends, as the mule-carriage began to recede from the fixed roller-beam, and to see them at leisure, after a few seconds' exercise of their tiny fingers, to amuse themselves in any attitude they chose, till the stretch and winding-on were once more completed. The work of these lively elves seemed to resemble a sport, in which habit gave them a pleasing dexterity. Conscious of their skill, they were delighted to show it off to any stranger. As to exhaustion by the day's work, they evinced no trace of it on emerging from the mill in the evening; for they immediately began to skip about any neighboring playground, and to commence their little amusements with the same alacrity as boys issuing from a school. It is moreover my firm conviction that if children are not ill-used by bad parents or guardians, but receive in food and raiment the full benefit of what they earn, they would thrive better when employed in our modern factories than if left at home in apartments too often ill aired, damp, and cold....

A LOW DEATH RATE

The mortality of that town* has diminished since 1801, at which time there were scarcely any manufactories established in it. The population of the township was in 1801, 30,669; and the burials of the three years preceding being 2882, or 941 annually, the resulting rate of mortality is one in thirty-two and a half. In 1831 the population was 71,602, and the burials of the three years preceding were 5153, or 1718 annually, giving a rate of mortality of one in forty-one and a half. Thus, since the comfortable wages of factory labor have begun to be enjoyed, the mortality has diminished in the proportion of thirty-two and a half to forty-one and a half; that is, only three persons die now, where four died in the golden age of precarious rural or domestic employment....

GOOD FOOD AND SANITATION

It seems established by a body of incontestable evidence that the wages of our factory work-people, if prudently spent, would enable them to live in a comfortable manner, and decidedly better than formerly, in consequence of the relative diminution in the price of food, fuel, lodgings, and clothing....

And as to the charge which has been made of the injury done to their constitutions by entering a factory in early life, the following refutation of it is most decisive. "There is one thing I feel convinced of from observation, that young persons, especially females, who have begun mill-work at from ten to twelve, independently of their becoming much more expert artists, preserve their health better, and possess sounder feet and legs

*Leeds, an industrial town in Northern England.

25

at twenty-five than those who have commenced from thirteen to sixteen and upwards.''

''At the Blantyre mills,'' says the same competent observer, ''the spinners are all males. I visited the dwellings of nine of that class without making any selection. Found that every one of them was married, and that the wife had been in every instance a mill-girl, some of these women having begun factory work as early as at six and a half years of age. The number of children born to these nine couples was fifty one; the number now living forty-six. As many of these children as are able to work, and can find vacancies, are employed in the mill. They all live in rooms rented from the owners, and are well lodged. I saw them at breakfast time, and the meal was composed of the following: viz., porridge and milk for the children; coffee, eggs, bread, oaten cake, and butter for the father.''...

England:
The Worker's Hell

Frederick Engels

A German-born economist and socialist,
Frederick Engels (1820-1895), along with Karl
Marx, was the dominant figure in the 19th
century communist movement. Engels was
converted to communism at the age of 21 by
Moses Hess, a leading German intellectual.
Engels moved to England, where he identified
himself with trade unions and radical reform
movements. An industrialist in his early years,
he withdrew from business in 1844 and began a
lifelong association with Marx. Upon Marx's
death, he completed, edited, and published
many of Marx's works, including volumes II and
III of *Das Kapital*. In the following reading,
Engels offers an account of the depressed
condition of England's working classes.

Consider the following questions while reading:

1. What was England like before the Machine Age?
2. How are working conditions in England after the machine
   age described by Engels?
3. What did the report of the Central Commission say?

Frederick Engels, **The Conditions of the Working Class** (Hemel Hempstead, England: George
Allen & Unwin Ltd., 1925), pp. 3-4, 19, 72, 67-70, 101. Reprinted with permission.

ENGLAND BEFORE THE MACHINE AGE

The history of the proletariat in England begins with the second half of the last century,* with the invention of the steam-engine and of machinery for working cotton. These inventions gave rise, as is well known, to an industrial revolution, a revolution which altered the whole civil society; one, the historical importance of which is only now beginning to be recognised. England is the classic soil of this transformation, which was all the mightier, the more silently it proceeded; and England is, therefore, the classic land of its chief product also, the proletariat. Only in England can the proletariat be studied in all its relations and from all sides....

Before the introduction of machinery, the spinning and weaving of raw materials was carried on in the workingman's home. Wife and daughter spun the yarn that the father wove or that they sold, if he did not work it up himself. These weaver families lived in the country in the neighborhood of the towns, and could get on fairly well with their wages....So it was that the weaver was usually in a position to lay by something and rent a little piece of land that he cultivated in his leisure hours, of which he had as many as he chose to take, since he could weave whenever and as long as he pleased. True, he was a bad farmer and managed his land inefficiently, often obtaining but poor crops; nevertheless, he was no proletarian, he had a stake in the country, he was permanently settled, and stood one step higher in society than the English workman of today.

So the workers vegetated throughout a passably comfortable existence, leading a righteous and peaceful life in all piety and probity; and their material position was far better than that of their successors. They did not need to overwork; they did no more than they chose to do, and yet earned what they needed. They had leisure for healthful work in garden or field, work which, in itself, was recreation for them, and they could take part besides in the recreations and games of their neighbors, and all these games, bowling, cricket, football, etc., contributed to their physical health and vigor. They were, for the most part, strong, well-built people, in whose physique little or no difference from that of their peasant neighbors was discoverable. Their children grew up in the fresh country air and,

*The 18th Century.

if they could help their parents at work, it was only occasionally; while of eight or twelve hours work for them there was no question....

CRUELTY TOWARD CHILDREN

The report of the Central Commission relates that the manufacturers began to employ children rarely of five years, often of six, very often of seven, usually of eight to nine years; that the working-day often lasted fourteen to sixteen hours, exclusive of meals and intervals; that the manufacturers permitted overlookers to flog and maltreat children, and often took an active part in so doing themselves. One case is related of a Scotch manufacturer who rode after a sixteen years old runaway, forced him to return running before the employer as fast as the master's horse trotted, and beat him the whole way with a long whip....

A HIGH DEATH RATE

Every great city has one or more slums where the working class is crowded together. True, poverty often dwells in hidden alleys close to the palaces of the rich; but, in general, a separate territory has been assigned to it, where, removed from the sight of the happier classes, it may struggle along as it can. These slums are pretty equally arranged in all the great towns of England, the worst houses in the worst quarters of the towns; usually one or two-storied cottages in long rows, perhaps with cellars used as dwellings, almost always irregularly built. These houses of three or four rooms and a kitchen form, throughout England, some parts of London excepted, the general dwellings of the working class. The streets are generally unpaved, rough, dirty, filled with vegetable and animal refuse, without sewers or gutters, but supplied with foul stagnant pools instead. Moreover, ventilation is impeded by the bad, confused method of building of the whole quarter, and since many human beings here live crowded into a small space, the atmosphere that prevails in these working-men's quarters may readily be imagined....

The death rate is kept so high chiefly by the heavy mortality among young children in the working class. The tender frame of a child is least able to withstand the unfavorable influences of an inferior lot in life; the neglect to which they are often subjected, when both parents work or one is dead, avenges itself promptly, and no one need wonder that in Manchester, according to the report last quoted, more than fifty-seven per cent of the children of the working class and not quite thirty-two per cent of the children of all classes in the country die under five years of age....

The social system in which a man, willing to work, is compelled to starve, is a blasphemy, an anarchy, and no system.

Thomas Devin Reilly, **The Irish Felon.**

POOR FOOD AND SANITATION

When one remembers under what conditions the working people live, when one thinks how crowded their dwellings are, how every nook and corner swarms with human beings, how sick and well sleep in the same room, in the same bed, the only wonder is that a contagious disease like this fever does not spread yet further....

Another category of diseases arises directly from the food rather than the dwellings of the workers. The food of the laborer, indigestible enough in itself, is utterly unfit for young children, and he has neither means nor time to get his children more suitable food....Scrofula is almost universal among the working class, and scrofulous parents have scrofulous children, especially when the original influences continue in full force to operate upon the inherited tendency of the children. How greatly all these evils are increased by the chances to which the workers are subject in consequence of fluctuations in trade, want of work, and the scanty wages of times of crisis, it is not necessary to dwell upon. Temporary want of sufficient food, to which almost every workingman is exposed at least once in the course of his life, only contributes to intensify the effects of his usual sufficient but bad diet. Children who are half starved just when they most need ample and nutritious food — and how many such there are during every crisis and even when trade is at its best — must inevitably become weak, scrofulous, and rachitic in a high degree. And that they do become so, their appearance amply shows. The neglect to which the great mass of workingmen's children are condemned leaves ineradicable traces and brings the enfeeblement of the whole race of workers with it. Add to this the unsuitable clothing of this class, the impossibility of precautions against colds, the necessity of toiling so long as health permits, want made more dire when sickness appears and the only too common lack of all medical assistance; and we have a rough idea of the sanitary condition of the English working class....

The Merit
of Self-Help

Samuel Smiles

A biographer and essayist, Samuel Smiles
(1812-1904) was Scotland's answer to Horatio
Alger. Virtually all of his works echo the same
simple theme: ''If at first you don't succeed,
try, try again.'' Smiles was convinced that any
individual of his day, through perseverance and
courage, could find success. In the following
viewpoint, he explains why ''self-help'' is the
best means possible of bettering oneself.

Consider the following questions while reading:

1. What is the root of individual growth and national strength?
2. How should the government behave?

Samuel Smiles, **Self-Help, With Illustrations of Character** (New York: Harper & Row, 1874), pp.
21-23, 25.

THE VALUE OF SELF-HELP

"Heaven helps those who help themselves" is a well-tried maxim, embodying in a small compass the results of vast human experience. The spirit of self-help is the root of all genuine growth in the individual; and, exhibited in the lives of many, it constitutes the true source of national vigor and strength. Help from without is often enfeebling in its effects, but help from within invariably invigorates. Whatever is done *for* men or classes, to a certain extent takes away the stimulus and necessity of doing for themselves; and where men are subjected to overguidance and over-government, the inevitable tendency is to render them comparatively helpless.

Even the best institutions can give a man no active help. Perhaps the most they can do is, to leave him free to develop himself and improve his individual condition. But in all times men have been prone to believe that their happiness and well-being were to be secured by means of institutions rather than by their own conduct. Hence the value of legislation as an agent in human advancement has usually been much over-estimated. To constitute the millionth part of a Legislature, by voting for one or two men once in three or five years, however conscientiously this duty may be performed, can exercise but little active influence upon any man's life and character. Moreover, it is every day becoming more clearly understood, that the function of Government is negative and restrictive, rather than positive and active; being resolvable principally into protection — protection of life, liberty, and property. Laws, wisely administered, will secure men in the enjoyment of the fruits of their labor, whether of mind or body, at a comparatively small personal sacrifice; but no laws, however stringent, can make the idle industrious, the thriftless provident, or the drunken sober. Such reforms can only be effected by means of individual action, economy, and self-denial; by better habits, rather than by greater rights.

NO GOVERNMENT INTERFERENCE

The Government of a nation itself is usually found to be but the reflex of the individuals composing it. The Government that is ahead of the people will inevitably be dragged down to their level, as the Government that is behind them will in the long run be dragged up. In the order of nature, the collective character of a nation will as surely find its befitting results in its law and government, as water finds its own level. The noble people will be nobly ruled, and the ignorant and corrupt ignobly. Indeed, all experience serves to prove that the worth and strength of a State depend far less upon the form of its institutions than upon the character of its men. For the nation is only an aggregate of individual conditions, and civilization itself is but a question of the personal improvement of the men, women, and children of whom society is composed.

All work, even cotton-spinning, is noble; work is alone noble.

Thomas Carlyle, **Past and Present**, 1, 1843.

National progress is the sum of individual industry, energy, and uprightness, as national decay is of individual idleness, selfishness, and vice. What we are accustomed to decry as great social evils, will for the most part be found to be but the outgrowth of man's own perverted life; and though we may endeavor to cut them down and extirpate them by means of Law, they will only spring up again with fresh luxuriance in some other form, unless the conditions of personal life and character are radically improved. If this view be correct, then it follows that the highest patriotism and philanthropy consists, not so much in altering laws and modifying institutions, as in helping and stimulating men to elevate and improve themselves by their own free and independent individual action.

It may be of comparatively little consequence how a man is governed from without, whilst every thing depends upon how he governs himself from within. The greatest slave is not he who is ruled by a despot, great though that evil be, but he who is the thrall of his own moral ignorance, selfishness, and vice. Nations who are thus enslaved at heart can not be freed by any mere changes of masters or of institutions....The solid Foundation of liberty must rest upon individual character; which is also the only sure guaranty for social security and national progress. John Stuart Mill truly observes that ''even despotism does not produce its worst effects so long as individuality exists under it; and whatever crushes individuality is despotism, by whatever name it be called.''

Viewpoint

The Need For Governmental Help

The Sadler Committee

The deplorable working conditions in England's mines and factories early in the 19th century prompted a series of parliamentary investigations. Several committees were formed to inquire into the gravity of the situation, especially where it concerned women and children. The findings of these committees created a scandal which shocked Parliament into enacting factory legislation aimed at correcting the abuses. The following testimony of two workers was presented in evidence before the Sadler Committee in 1832.

No questions for discussion needed.

Raymond Phineas, **Pageant of Europe**, (New York: Harcourt, Brace & World, Inc., 1961), pp. 493-95. Reprinted with permission.

MR. MATTHEW CRABTREE, CALLED IN; AND EXAMINED

What age are you? — Twenty-two.

What is your occupation? — A blanket manufacturer.

Have you ever been employed in a factory? — Yes.

At what age did you first go to work in one? — Eight.

How long did you continue in that occupation? — Four years.

Will you state the hours of labour at the period when you first went to the factory, in ordinary times? — From 6 in the morning to 8 at night.

Fourteen hours? — Yes.

With what intervals for refreshment and rest? — An hour at noon.

When trade was brisk what were your hours? — From 5 in the morning to 9 in the evening.

Sixteen hours? — Yes....

How far did you live from the mill? — About two miles.

Was there any time allowed for you to get your breakfast in the mill? — No.

Did you take it before you left your home? — Generally.

During those long hours of labour could you be punctual; how did you awake? — I seldom did awake spontaneously; I was most generally awoke or lifted out of bed, sometimes asleep, by my parents.

Were you always in time? — No.

What was the consequence if you had been too late? — I was most commonly beaten.

Severely? — Very severely, I thought.

In those mills is chastisement towards the latter part of the day going on perpetually? — Perpetually.

So that you can hardly be in a mill without hearing constant crying? — Never an hour, I believe.

Do you think that if the overlooker were naturally a humane person it would be still found necessary for him to beat the children, in order to keep up their attention and vigilance at the termination of those extraordinary days of labour? — Yes; the machine turns off a regular quantity of cardings, and of course they must keep as regularly to their work the whole of the day; they must keep with the machine, and therefore however humane the slubber may be, as he must keep up with the machine or be found fault with, he spurs the children to keep up also by various means but that which he commonly resorts to is to strap them when they become drowsy.

At the time when you were beaten for not keeping up with your work, were you anxious to have done it if you possibly could? — Yes; the dread of being beaten if we could not keep up with our work was a sufficient impulse to keep us to it if we could.

When you got home at night after this labour, did you feel much fatigued? — Very much so.

Had you any time to be with your parents, and to receive instruction from them? — No.

What did you do? — All that we did when we got home was to get the little bit of supper that was provided for us and go to bed immediately. If the supper had not been ready directly, we should have gone to sleep while it was preparing.

Did you not, as a child, feel it a very grievous hardship to be roused so soon in the morning? — I did.

Were the rest of the children similarly circumstanced? — Yes, all of them; but they were not all of them so far from their work as I was.

A STATE OF SLAVERY

Let the truth speak out, appalling as the statements may appear. Thousands of our fellow-creatures and fellow-subjects ...are at this very moment existing in a state of slavery more horrid than are the victims of that hellish system, colonial slavery....Thousands of little children...are daily compelled to labor from 6 o'clock in the morning to 7 o'clock in the evening with only — British, blush while you read it — with only 30 minutes allowed for eating and recreation.

Richard Oastler, **Slavery in Yorkshire.**

And if you had been too late you were under the apprehension of being cruelly beaten? — I generally was beaten, when I happened to be too late; and when I got up in the morning the apprehension of that was so great, that I used to run, and cry all the way as I went to the mill.

THE EVIDENCE OF SAMUEL COULSON

At what time in the morning, in the brisk time, did those girls go to the mills? — In the brisk time, for about six weeks, they have gone at 3 o'clock in the morning, and ended at 10, or nearly half-past, at night.

What intervals were allowed for rest or refreshment during those nineteen hours of labour? — Breakfast a quarter of an hour, and dinner half an hour, and drinking a quarter of an hour....

Had you not great difficulty in awakening your children to this excessive labour? — Yes, in the early time we had them to take up asleep and shake them, when we got them on the floor to dress them, before we could get them off to their work; but not so in the common hours.

Supposing they had been a little too late, what would have been the consequence during the long hours? — They were quartered in the longest hours the same as in the shortest time.

What do you mean by quartering? — A quarter taken off.

If they had been how much too late? — Five minutes.

What was the length of time they could be in bed during those long hours? — It was near 11 o'clock before we could get them into bed after getting a little victuals, and then at morning my mistress used to stop up all night, for fear we could not get them ready for the time; sometimes we have gone to bed, and one of us generally awoke.

What time did you get them up in the morning? — In general me or my mistress got up at 2 o'clock to dress them.

So that they had not above four hours sleep at this time? — No, they had not.

For how long together was it? — About six weeks it held; it was done only when the throng was very much on; it was not often that.

The common hours of labour were from 6 in the morning till half-past eight at night? — Yes.

With the same intervals for food? — Yes, just the same.

Were the children excessively fatigued by this labour? — Many times; we have cried often when we have given them the little victualling we had to give them; we had to shake them, and they have fallen asleep with the victuals in their mouths many a time.

Had any of them any accident in consequence of this labour? — Yes, my eldest daughter...the cog caught her forefinger nail and screwed it off below the knuckle, and she was five weeks in the Leeds infirmary.

Has she lost that finger? — It is cut off at the second joint.

Were her wages paid during that time? — As soon as the accident happened the wages were totally stopped; indeed, I did not know which way to get her cured....

Did this excessive term of labour occasion much cruelty also?
— Yes, with being so much fatigued the strap was very frequently used.

Have any of your children been strapped? — Yes, every one; the eldest daughter; I was up in Lancashire a fortnight, and when I got home I saw her shoulders, and I said, "Ann, what is the matter?" She said, "the overlooker has strapped me; but," she said, "do not go to the overlooker, for if you do we shall lose our work."…Her back was beat nearly to a jelly….

What was the wages in the short hours? — Three shillings a week each.

When they wrought those very long hours what did they get? — Three shillings and sevenpence halfpenny.

For all that additional labour they had only 7½ pence a week additional? — No more.

At one time children formed one third of the industrial labor force in America. Young boys working at midnight in Indiana glassworks, 1908. Wide World Photos

In Defense
of Wealth

Andrew Carnegie

Andrew Carnegie (1835-1919) presents one of
the most extraordinary success stories in
American history. A Scottish immigrant, he was
a laborer in a cotton factory, a messenger for a
telegraph company, and a railroad worker
before eventually becoming the leading iron
and steel manufacturer in the United States.
Carnegie was a shrewd businessman who
possessed a boundless and unwavering faith in
America as a land of opportunity. His success as
an industrialist was equaled by his generosity
as a philanthropist. Convinced that the wealthy
had a responsibility to society, Carnegie was
directly responsible for the creation of philanthropic foundations worth in excess of one
billion dollars. In the following reading, he
attempts to explain and justify the great dispar-
ity of wealth among people.

Consider the following questions while reading:

1. What revolutionary changes have taken place?
2. What price does society have to pay for these changes and
   why should society accept this price?
3. How does Andrew Carnegie define human nature?

Andrew Carnegie, ''Wealth,'' **North American Review**, June 1889, pp. 653-57.

A REVOLUTIONARY CHANGE

The conditions of human life have not only been changed, but revolutionized, within the past few hundred years. In former days there was little difference between the dwelling, dress, food, and environment of the chief and those of his retainers... The contrast between the palace of the millionaire and the cottage of the laborer with us to-day measures the change which has come with civilization.

The change, however, is not to be deplored, but welcomed as highly beneficial. It is well, nay, essential for the progress of the race, that the houses of some should be homes for all that is highest and best in literature and the arts, and for all the refinements of civilization, rather than that none should be so. Much better this great irregularity than universal squalor...But whether the change be for good or ill, it is upon us, beyond our power to alter, and therefore to be accepted and made the best of. It is a waste of time to criticise the inevitable....

THE PRICE OF CHANGE

The price we pay for this salutary change is, no doubt, great. We assemble thousands of operatives in the factory, in the mine, and in the counting-house, of whom the employer is little better than a myth. All intercourse between them is at an end. Rigid Castes are formed, and, as usual, mutual ignorance breeds mutual distrust. Each Caste is without sympathy for the other, and ready to credit anything disparaging in regard to it. Under the law of competition, the employer of thousands is forced into the strictest economies, among which the rates paid to labor figures prominently, and often there is friction between the employer and the employed, between capital and labor, between rich and poor. Human society loses homogeneity.

The price which society pays for the law of competition, like the price it pays for cheap comforts and luxuries, is also great; but the advantages of this law are also greater still, for it is to this law that we owe our wonderful material development, which brings improved conditions in its train. But, whether the law be benign or not, we must say of it, as we say of the change in the conditions of men to which we have referred: It is here; we cannot evade it; no substitutes for it have been found; and while the law may be sometimes hard for the individual, it is best for the race, because it insures the survival of the fittest in every department. We accept and welcome, therefore, as conditions to which we must accommodate ourselves, great inequality of environment, the concentration of business, industrial and commercial, in the hands of a few, and the law of competition between these, as being not only beneficial, but essential for the future progress of the race....

CAPITAL IS GOOD

Capital is good; the capitalist is a helper, if he is not also a monopolist. We can safely let any one get as rich as he can if he will not despoil others in doing so.

Henry George, **Social Problems**.

THE LAW OF NATURE

Objections to the foundations upon which society is based are not in order, because the condition of the race is better with these than it has been with any others which have been tried. Of the effect of any new substitutes proposed we cannot be sure. The Socialist or Anarchist who seeks to overturn present conditions is to be regarded as attacking the foundation upon which civilization itself rests, for civilization took its start from the day that the capable, industrious workman said to his incompetent and lazy fellow, "If thou dost not sow, thou shalt not reap," and thus ended primitive Communism by separating the drones from the bees...Good has come to the race from the accumulation of wealth by those who have the ability and energy that produce it. But even if we admit for a moment that it might be better for the race to discard its present foundation, Individualism, — that it is a nobler ideal that man should labor, not for himself alone, but in and for a brotherhood of his fellows, and share with them all in common, realizing Swedenborg's idea of Heaven, where, as he says, the angels derive their happiness, not from laboring for self, but for each other, — even admit all this, and a sufficient answer is, This is not evolution, but revolution. It necessitates the changing of human nature itself — a work of aeons, even if it were good to

43

change it, which we cannot know. It is not practicable in our day or in our age. Even if desirable theoretically, it belongs to another and long-succeeding sociological stratum. Our duty is with what is practicable now; with the next step possible in our day and generation. It is criminal to waste our energies in endeavoring to uproot, when all we can profitably or possibly accomplish is to bend the universal tree of humanity a little in the direction most favorable to the production of good fruit under existing circumstances. We might as well urge the destruction of the highest existing type of man because he failed to reach our ideal as to favor the destruction of Individualism, Private Property, the Law of Accumulation of Wealth, and the Law of Competition; for these are the highest results of human experience, the soil in which society so far has produced the best fruit. Unequally or unjustly, perhaps, as these laws sometimes operate, and imperfect as they appear to the Idealist, they are, nevertheless, like the highest type of man, the best and most valuable of all that humanity has yet accomplished.

Andrew Carnegie rose from poverty to become a steel tycoon and philanthropist. United Press International, Inc.

In Defence
of Socialism

Upton Sinclair

Upton Sinclair (1878-1968) was an American
author who actively crusaded against the social
and economic ills in the United States. Born in
Baltimore, Maryland of a prominent but impoverished family, he supported himself while in
college by writing dime novels. Sinclair devoted
his adult life to the cause of socialism and, in
1934, was nearly elected governor of California
on his socialistic EPIC (End Poverty In California) platform. The majority of his novels
dealt with anti-establishment themes. His most
famous work, *The Jungle*, is an exposé of
conditions in the Chicago meat-packing
industry at the turn of the century. The following excerpt from that book describes the plight
of Jurgis, a Lithuanian immigrant, during his
first days of work at the infamous fertilizer
plant.

Consider the following questions while reading:

1. How is the fertilizer plant described?
2. What kind of work did Jurgis perform in the fertilizer plant?

Upton Sinclair, **The Jungle** (New York: New American Library, 1905), pp. 128-32. By permission
of Bertha Klausner International Literary Agency, Inc.

A FEARFUL PLACE

All this while that he was seeking for work, there was a dark shadow hanging over Jurgis; as if a savage beast were lurking somewhere in the pathway of his life, and he knew it, and yet could not help approaching the place. There are all stages of being out of work in Packingtown, and he faced in dread the prospect of reaching the lowest. There is a place that waits for the lowest man — the fertilizer plant!

The men would talk about it in awe-stricken whispers. Not more than one in ten had ever really tried it; the other nine had contented themselves with hearsay evidence and a peep through the door. There were some things worse than even starving to death. They would ask Jurgis if he had worked there yet, and if he meant to; and Jurgis would debate the matter with himself. As poor as they were, and making all the sacrifices that they were, would he dare to refuse any sort of work that was offered to him, be it as horrible as ever it could? Would he dare to go home and eat bread that had been earned by Ona, weak and complaining as she was, knowing that he had been given a chance, and had not the nerve to take it? — And yet he might argue that way with himself all day, and one glimpse into the fertilizer works would send him away again shuddering. He was a man, and he would do his duty; he went and made application — but surely he was not also required to hope for success!

THE FERTILIZER PLANT

The fertilizer works of Durham's lay away from the rest of the plant. Few visitors ever saw them, and the few who did would come out looking like Dante, of whom the peasants declared that he had been into hell. To this part of the yards came all the ''tankage,'' and the waste products of all sorts; here they dried out the bones — and in suffocating cellars where the daylight never came you might see men and women and children bending over whirling machines and sawing bits of bone into all sorts of shapes, breathing their lungs full of the fine dust, and doomed to die, every one of them, within a certain definite time. Here they made the blood into albumen, and made other foul-smelling things into things still more foul-smelling. In the corridors and caverns where it was done you might lose yourself as in the great caves of Kentucky. In the dust and the steam the electric lights would shine like far-off twinkling stars — red and blue, green and purple stars, according to the color of the mist and the brew from which it came. For the odors in these ghastly charnel houses there may be words in Lithuanian, but there are none in English. The person entering would have to summon his courage as for a cold-water plunge. He would go on like a man swimming under water; he would put his handkerchief over his face, and begin to cough and choke; and then, if he were still obstinate, he would find his head beginning to ring, and the veins in his forehead to throb, until finally he would be assailed by an overpowering blast of ammonia fumes, and would turn and run for his life, and come out half-dazed.

On top of this were the rooms where they dried the "tankage," the mass of brown stringy stuff that was left after the waste portions of the carcasses had had the lard and tallow dried out of them. This dried material they would then grind to a fine powder, and after they had mixed it up well with a mysterious but inoffensive brown rock which they brought in and ground up by the hundreds of carloads for that purpose, the substance was ready to be put into bags and sent out to the world as any one of a hundred different brands of standard bone phosphate. And then the farmer in Maine or California or Texas would buy this, at say twenty-five dollars a ton, and plant it with his corn; and for several days after the operation the fields would have a strong odor, and the farmer and his wagon and the very horses that had hauled it would all have it too. In Packingtown the fertilizer is pure, instead of being a flavoring, and instead of a ton or so spread out on several acres under the open sky, there are hundreds and thousands of tons of it in one building, heaped here and there in haystack piles, covering the floor several inches deep, and filling the air with a choking dust that becomes a blinding sand storm when the wind stirs.

INHUMAN LABOR

It was to this building that Jurgis came daily, as if dragged by an unseen hand. The month of May was an exceptionally cool one, and his secret prayers were granted; but early in June there came a record-breaking hot spell, and after that there were men wanted in the fertilizer mill.

The boss of the grinding room had come to know Jurgis by this time, and had marked him for a likely man; and so when he came to the door about two o'clock this breathless hot day, he felt a sudden spasm of pain shoot through him — the boss beckoned to him! In ten minutes more Jurgis had pulled off his coat and overshirt, and set his teeth together and gone to work. Here was one more difficulty for him to meet and conquer!

His labor took him about one minute to learn. Before him was one of the vents of the mill in which the fertilizer was being ground — rushing forth in a great brown river, with a spray of the finest dust flung forth in clouds. Jurgis was given a shovel, and along with half a dozen others it was his task to shovel this fertilizer into carts. That others were at work he knew by the sound, and by the fact that he sometimes collided with them; otherwise they might as well not have been there, for in the blinding dust storm a man could not see six feet in front of his face. When he had filled one cart he had to grope around him until another came, and if there was none on hand he continued to grope till one arrived. In five minutes he was, of course, a mass of fertilizer from head to feet; they gave him a sponge to tie over his mouth, so that he could breathe, but the sponge did not prevent his lips and eyelids from caking up with it and his ears from filling solid. He looked like a brown ghost at twilight — from hair to shoes he became the color of the building and of everything in it, and for that matter a hundred yards outside it. The building had to be left open, and when the wind blew Durham and Company lost a great deal of fertilizer.

CONFESSIONS OF A CAPITALIST

The work of the working people, and nothing else, produces the wealth, which, by some hocus-pocus arrangement, is transferred to me, leaving them bare. While they support me in splendid style, what do I do for them? Let the candid upholder of the present order answer, for I am not aware of doing anything for them.

Joseph Medill Patterson, **Confessions of a Drone.**

Working in his shirtsleeves, and with the thermometer at over a hundred, the phosphates soaked in through every pore of Jurgis's skin, and in five minutes he had a headache, and in fifteen was almost dazed. The blood was pounding in his brain like an engine's throbbing; there was a frightful pain in the top of his skull, and he could hardly control his hands. Still, with the memory of his four months' siege behind him, he fought on, in a frenzy of determination; and half an hour later he began to vomit — he vomited until it seemed as if his inwards must be torn into shreds. A man could get used to the fertilizer mill, the boss said, if he would only make up his mind to it; but Jurgis now began to see that it was a question of making up his stomach.

JURGIS ENDURES

At the end of that day of horror, he could scarcely stand. He had to catch himself now and then, and lean against a building and get his bearings. Most of the men, when they came out, made straight for a saloon — they seemed to place fertilizer and rattlesnake poison in one class. But Jurgis was too ill to think of drinking — he could only make his way to the street and stagger on to a car. He had a sense of humor, and later on, when he became an old hand, he used to think it fun to board a street car and see what happened. Now, however, he was too ill to notice it — how the people in the car began to gasp and sputter, to put their handkerchiefs to their noses, and transfix him with furious glances. Jurgis only knew that a man in front of him immediately got up and gave him a seat; and that half a minute later the two people on each side of him got up; and that in a full minute the crowded car was nearly empty — those passengers who could not get room on the platform having gotten out to walk.

Of course Jurgis had made his home a miniature fertilizer mill a minute after entering. The stuff was half an inch deep in his skin — his whole system was full of it, and it would have taken a week not merely of scrubbing, but of vigorous exercise, to get it out of him. As it was, he could be compared with nothing known to men, save that newest discovery of the savants, a substance which emits energy for an unlimited time, without being itself in the least diminished in power. He smelt so that he made all the food at the table taste, and set the whole family to vomiting; for himself it was three days before he could keep anything upon his stomach — he might wash his hands, and use a knife and fork, but were not his mouth and throat filled with the poison?

And still Jurgis stuck it out! In spite of splitting headaches he would stagger down to the plant and take up his stand once more, and begin to shovel in the blinding clouds of dust. And so at the end of the week he was a fertilizer man for life — he was able to eat again, and though his head never stopped aching, it ceased to be so bad that he could not work.

Exercise 2

Revolution and Change

The following exercise will explore your attitude toward change. Sometimes change brings progress, other times pain and suffering, and frequently both progress and human suffering are by-products of social, political, scientific, and technological change. Change can occur either slowly or suddenly (i.e., revolutionary change).

Consider each of the following circumstances carefully. Mark (G) whenever you feel gradual change is needed. Mark (R) for circumstances that you believe demand revolutionary change. And mark (S) if you think the status quo should be maintained (no change needed).

R = REVOLUTIONARY CHANGE NEEDED
G = GRADUAL CHANGE NEEDED
S = STATUS QUO SHOULD BE MAINTAINED

_____ 1. American foreign policy toward developing nations

_____ 2. U.S. policy toward Communist China

_____ 3. Crime and urban unrest in American cities

_____ 4. The status of women in society

_____ 5. The welfare programs

_____ 6. The military budget

_____ 7. The American economic system

_____ 8. Segregated public schools

_____ 9. Air and water pollution

_____ 10. Segregation of black and white neighborhoods

_____ 11. Social Security

_____ 12. Public education

_____ 13. Poverty in rural America

_____ 14. The status of Indians in American society

Chapter 3

Capitalism:

Capitalism Today:
For and Against

INTRODUCTION

The capitalistic system has changed considerably in the 20th century in the industrialized democratic nations of the world. The primary reason for this has been the ongoing transformation in the relationship between government and industry and between industry and labor. Government has been playing a larger and more visible role in the affairs of business. The proliferation of laws regulating monopolies, the pricing of goods, child labor, and minimum wage scales have succeeded in controlling or removing most of the excesses which characterized industry in the 19th century. Labor, for its part, has been effectively organizing. Through collective bargaining, unions have won higher wages, better working conditions, and generous fringe benefits for their members.

As a result of these and other changes in the marketplace, the basic arguments for and against capitalism have been updated to reflect contemporary conditions. While modern supporters still cling to Adam Smith's principle of laissez-faire, they have carried it a step further. Today's capitalists tend to be political conservatives who equate economic freedom with political freedom. Accordingly, many claim that when government is permitted to interfere in the economic affairs of a nation, not only will inefficiency in business result, but also an erosion of political freedom. On the reverse side, the recent upward surge in unemployment and inflation and the large pockets of poverty still existent in the industrialized democracies are offered as evidence of the failure and pending bankruptcy of capitalism. Moreover, even those workers enjoying a relatively high degree of affluence are small justification for the steady flow of huge corporate profits. Under the present system, it is argued, the worker never has, and never will, receive a fair share of the pie.

The following readings reflect the positions outlined above. The conservatives represented defend capitalism on the lofty grounds of human freedom; the opponents attack it from the tangible vantage of human need.

Viewpoint 9

Capitalism and Freedom

Perry Gresham

Educator and author Perry Gresham is President Emeritus of Bethany College, Bethany, West Virginia. Gresham was a director of the Foundation for Economic Education and is an honorary life member of the World Federation of Robert Burns Societies. A former feature writer with the *Detroit Free Press*, his published works include *For Individuals Only*, *Answer to Conformity*, and *Abiding Values*. In the following article, Gresham outlines what he perceives to be capitalism's most enduring strengths and concludes that no reasonable alternatives exist to replace it.

Consider the following questions while reading:

1. How is capitalism defined?
2. What is the record of capitalism?
3. How should the government and capitalism relate to each other?

Perry Gresham, "Think Twice Before You Disparage Capitalism," **The Freeman**, March 1977, pp. 132-34, 136-37.

IS THE SYSTEM OUTMODED?

Many thoughtful citizens of America think of capitalism as a quaint and vanishing vestige of our Yankee industrial beginnings. With burgeoning population, urbanization and industrialization, they argue, capitalism disappears. They are not quite ready to embrace socialism, but they heartily approve government planning and intervention. John Kenneth Galbraith, articulate spokesman for the liberal establishment, calls for the open acclaim of a new socialism which he believes to be both imminent and necessary. "The new socialism allows of no acceptable alternatives; it cannot be escaped except at the price of grave discomfort, considerable social disorder and, on occasion, lethal damage to health and well-being. The new socialism is not ideological; it is compelled by circumstance."

At first blush, the Marxian assumption of economic determinism is quite plausible, but I do not believe it can stand up to the scrutiny of experience. My study of history leads me to assume with many of my thoughtful colleagues that free people can, within certain limits, choose their own systems of political economy. This is precisely what happened in West Germany at the time of Ludwig Erhard. The Germans chose capitalism rather than the socialism recommended by many American, British, and Continental economists and politicians. It is my opinion that Americans can and should call for a renewal of capitalism rather than a new socialism.

EMPLOYEES SHOULD BE GRATEFUL

American employees should be very grateful for our private enterprise economy which allows them personal freedom and pays them the highest income that employees ever received.

George S. Benson, **Our American Heritage**.

Capitalism has been neither understood nor sympathetically considered by most contemporary Americans. Capitalism is a radical and appealing system of political economy which needs a new and favorable review. The new socialism has never been tried. The old socialism is not very inviting. Consider Russia,

China, Cuba, Chile, and now Britain. Capitalism has been tried with the most amazing success in all history. What is the nature of a political and economic system which has made the poor people of America more prosperous than the rich of many countries operating under State control? Here are my paragraphs in praise of capitalism. They are somewhat lyrical but grounded in fact and open to review.

AN ENVIABLE RECORD

Capitalism is the one system of political economy which works, has worked and, given a chance, will continue to work. The alternative system is socialism. Socialism is seductive in theory, but tends toward tyranny and serfdom in practice.

Capitalism was not born with *The Wealth of Nations*, nor will it die with *Das Kapital*. It is as old as history and as new as a paper route for a small boy. Capitalism is a point of view and a way of life. Its principles apply whether or not they are understood, approved and cherished.

Capitalism is no relic of Colonial America. It has the genius of freedom to change with the times and to meet the challenges of big industries, big unions, and big government if it can free itself from the restraints of interest-group intervention which eventuates in needless government expansion and spending. Let the market work, and the ambition of each individual will serve the common good of society.

Capitalism is an economic system which believes with Locke and Jefferson that life, liberty, and property are among the inalienable rights of man.

Capitalism denies the banal dichotomy between property values and human values. Property values *are* human values. Imagine the disjunction when it is applied to a person with a mechanical limb or a cardiac pacemaker. The workman with his tools and the farmer with his land are almost as dramatic in the exemplification of the identity between a person and his property.

Capitalism is belief in man — an assumption that prosperity and happiness are best achieved when each person lives by his

57

own will and his own intelligence. Each person is a responsible citizen.

LIMITED GOVERNMENT

✝ Capitalism recognizes the potential tyranny of any government. The government is made for man; not man for the government. Therefore, government should be limited in size and function, lest free individuals lose their identity, become wards of the State. Frederic Bastiat has called the State a "great fiction wherein everybody tries to live at the expense of everybody else."

Capitalism denies the naive and mystic faith in the State to control wages and prices. A fair price is the amount agreed upon by the buyer and seller. Competition in a free market is far more trustworthy than any government administrator. The government is a worthy defense against force and fraud, but the market is much better at protecting against monopoly, inflation, soaring prices, depressed wages and the problems of scarcity. Capitalism works to the advantage of consumer and worker alike.

✗ Capitalism denies the right of government to take the property of a private citizen at will, or to tax away his livelihood at will, or to tell him when and where he must work or how and where he must live. Capitalism is built on the firm foundation of individual liberty.

Capitalism believes that every person deserves an opportunity. "All men are created equal" in terms of opportunity, but people are not equal — nor should they be. How dull a world in which nobody could outrun anybody! Competition is a good thing no matter how much people try to avoid it. Equality and liberty are contradictory. Capitalism chooses liberty!

EQUALITY OF OPPORTUNITY

Capitalism gives a poor person an opportunity to become rich. It does not lock people into the condition of poverty. It calls on every individual to help his neighbor, but not to pauperize him with making him dependent. Independence for every person is the capitalist ideal.

When a person contracts to work for a day, a week, or a month before he is paid, he is practicing capitalism. It is a series of contracts for transactions to be completed in the future. Capitalism is promise and fulfillment.

Capitalism offers full employment to those who wish to work. The worker is free to accept a job at any wage he can get. He can join with his fellows in voluntary association to improve his salary and working conditions. He can change jobs or start his own business. He relies on his ability to perform rather than on the coercive power of the State to force his employment.

Capitalism is color-blind. Black, brown, yellow, red and white are alike in the market place. A person is regarded for his ability rather than his race. Economic rewards in the market place, like honor and acclaim on the playing field, are proportionate to performance. The person who has the most skill, ability and ingenuity to produce is paid accordingly by the people who value and need his goods and services....

Those who love liberty more than equality, those who are uneasy with unlimited government, those who have faith in man's ability to shape his own destiny, those who have marveled at the miracle of the market will join me in this call for renewal of this simple, reasonable, versatile and open system of capitalism which has worked, is working, and will work if freed from the fetters of limitless state intervention. The choice, I believe, is ours. The alternative is the stifling sovereign state.

Viewpoint 10

Socialism and Freedom

Jules Levin

Jules Levin was the Socialist Labor Party candidate for President in 1976. The following statement was prepared by Levin during the campaign for broadcast by the CBS radio network. He stresses that the ''capitalist system is in a general crisis,'' with unemployment and inflation being symptoms of this. Capitalism, he feels, should be replaced by a new economic order in which the economy is ''brought under the full control of the workers.''

Consider the following questions while reading:

1. How is the problem of unemployment described?
2. Why is capitalism in a state of decline?
3. For what reasons is socialism presented as a real alternative to capitalism?

Jules Levin, ''Levin Speaks for Socialism,'' **Weekly People**, October 9, 1976. Reprinted with permission.

In the last couple of years, many of us workers have experienced some especially hard times. We have just been through the worst economic recession since the Great Depression of the 1930's. Jobs have been hard, if not impossible, to find. Where we do have a job, the bosses have been piling on more and more work, forcing us to work faster as well as harder. At the same time, prices of food, clothing, shelter and other necessities have been going up faster than our paychecks. And the situation is not getting any better.

CAPITALIST "RECOVERY"

I am aware that since early last spring, we have been flooded with reports about a so-called economic recovery.

Sure enough a recovery of sorts has taken place. It hasn't helped many of us workers, but it has filled the coffers of the giant corporations and their owners. It is a recovery that can be summed up in a few words: higher profits for the capitalists.

During the second quarter of 1976, profits spurted up an average of 33 percent over the same period last year. At General Motors they were up 273 percent; at Ford they soared 400 percent; at Du Pont de Nemours, 430 percent; at Corning Glass Works, 331 percent; and so on. This is what the current economic recovery is all about.

We can sum it up by saying that the recovery hasn't helped our paychecks stretch further at the supermarkets, nor has it put the millions of workers out pounding the pavement back to work.

In fact, while the profits of the capitalists have skyrocketed, the living standards of workers have declined. This decline may be measured in a general way by the deteriorating quality of life in America — by the pollution, the urban decay, and the host of other social problems that affect all of us.

But this decline may be measured more precisely by the fall in the buying power of our wages. The official figures on this score should surprise no one. According to the Labor Department's Bureau of Labor Statistics, real takehome pay in the month of August, adjusted for consumer price increases since

61

1967, was lower than in 1968. In other words, we aren't as well off now as we were last year or even eight years ago.

CLASS CONFLICT

The working class and the employing class have nothing in common. There can be no peace so long as hunger and want are found among millions of working people, and the few who make up the employing class have all the good things of life.

Industrial Workers of the World, Preamble to the Constitution, adopted at Chicago, June 27, 1905.

UNEMPLOYMENT INCREASES

Some of us are far worse off mainly because we can't find a job. In spite of the so-called economic recovery, unemployment has steadily risen in the last three months. Officially the unemployment rate in August was reported as 7.9 percent.

Unofficially it is admitted that the jobless rate is much higher. In some areas it is equal to or even surpasses the unemployment rate during the Great Depression.

Here are some unemployment figures that are shocking:

Thirty percent of the building trades workers in New York are out of work, according to Peter Brennan, president of the New York State and City Building and Construction Trades Councils.

In New York City, 45 percent of the workers in the ladies garment field can't find work, E. Howard Milisani, a Ladies Garment Union official and secretary-treasurer of New York State's AFL-CIO, reported recently.

Unemployment among black youths now runs 40 percent and more in some communities.

Where are the needed jobs going to come from? From private industry? But private industry hasn't hired more workers because it has no place to sell what they produce.

62

Nothing short of a massive economic expansion can create the millions of jobs needed to put the unemployed to work, but barring a new war, there is no economic factor in sight that can be expected to create the new markets needed to stimulate production and provide those jobs....

HISTORICAL DECLINE

Let's be blunt. The capitalist system is in a general crisis, marked by chronic unemployment on the one hand and inflation on the other.

And let's not be deceived by illusions that the situation is going to get better. There may be economic fluctuations. And there may even be an occasional temporary upturn. But in the long term, we have entered a period of economic stagnation and decline.

Today, the capitalist class is desperately trying to save its privileged position in society. The meaning of this for the vast majority of Americans is clear — more austerity, and more belt tightening. And that's not all.

To keep itself in power and to maintain its class rule, the capitalist class is turning more and more to police state measures. The attacks on civil liberties during recent years have not been the work of demented individuals. They are the acts of a desperate ruling class confronted with a collapsing social system.

The picture of the future under capitalism is not bright. But I believe the current trend toward disaster can be halted and that we can find a new path of progress. However, that is possible only if the workers take far-reaching measures — measures that most of you probably have never seriously considered....

SOCIALISM: A REAL ALTERNATIVE

First, we must scrap that which is now a hindrance to our further progress — the capitalist system.

Second, in its place we must build a new social system, one that will lay the foundation for economic democracy and economic security, a society in which we will produce to satisfy the wants and needs of all the people instead of for the profit of the owning few. To do that the economy must be brought under the full control of the workers — those who produce all the social wealth and perform all the social services — organized into an industrial form of government. Or to put it more succinctly, we must establish a socialist society.

Socialism is the collective ownership by all the people of the factories, mills, mines, railroads, land and all other instruments of production. Socialism means production to satisfy human needs and it means direct control and management of the industries and social services by the workers through a democratic government based on their nationwide economic organization.

Under socialism, all authority will originate from the workers, integrally united in socialist industrial unions. In each workplace, the rank and file will elect whatever committees or representatives are needed to facilitate production. Within each shop or office division of a plant, the rank and file will participate directly in formulating and implementing all plans necessary for efficient operations.

STEPPING STONE TO REACTION

Reprinted by permission of the Weekly People

Besides electing all necessary shop officers, the workers will also elect representatives to a local and national council of their industry or service — and to a central congress representing all the industries and services. This all-industrial congress will plan and coordinate production in all areas of the economy.

ECONOMIC FREEDOM

All persons elected to any post in the socialist government, from the lowest to the highest level, will be directly accountable to the rank and file. They will be subject to removal at any time that a majority of those who elected them decide it is necessary.

Such a system would make possible the fullest democracy and freedom. It would be a society based on the most primary freedom — economic freedom.

For individuals, socialism means an end to economic insecurity and exploitation. It means workers cease to be commodities bought and sold on the labor market, and forced to work as appendages to tools owned by someone else. It means a chance to develop all individual capacities and potentials within a free community of free individuals. It means a classless society that guarantees full democratic rights for all workers.

The Virtues
of Capitalism

Lawrence Fertig

Born and educated in New York City, Lawrence
Fertig is a syndicated economic columnist and
practicing businessman. He is a widely known
and respected economist and a member of the
Board of Trustees of New York University. The
following reading is taken from his book,
Prosperity Through Freedom. In it, Fertig
argues that under socialism human rights will
be diminished, since political and economic
freedom are indivisible.

Consider the following questions while reading:

1. How is capitalism defined?
2. What is the danger of collectivism?
3. How is a traditional liberal different from a new-day liberal?

Lawrence Fertig, **Prosperity Through Freedom** (Chicago: Henry Regnery Co., 1961), pp. 3-11.
Reprinted with permission from Contemporary Books, Inc.

What are the virtues of a free enterprise economy? Why is private capitalism of such great value to the American citizen that he should defend it to the death against communism? It is the *only* system which can achieve the following objectives:

"HUMAN FREEDOM"

Human Freedom — Any economic system which does not accomplish this is bad, no matter what advantages are claimed for it. For over five thousand years people have struggled to get their rulers off their backs, and it would be tragic if we retraced our steps. John Chamberlain in his *Roots of Capitalism* has stated the case well in the following paragraph: "There are so many spiritual implications in liberty that it deserves to be considered an end in itself. Even if State planning offered more material goods, people who have known and cherished liberty would rather live as free human beings on a more modest standard of living than sell their birth-right for a mess of totalitarian pottage. But no such alternative exists. The fruits of totalitarianism are for the State, at most for a limited class."...

Political liberty and economic freedom are intertwined — they cannot be separated. Any system which deprives the individual of his economic freedom — by controlling his job, or how much he can earn, or what he can earn, or what he should buy, or how he should live — takes away his basic freedom. And it is important to remember that throughout history, whenever bureaucrats controlled people's economic lives, they soon came to control their political freedom as well. It is essential for the survival of democratic government that economic power be separated from political power. This is the sine qua non of democracy. It is the reason why the preservation of private capitalism is essential for the maintenance of a free society....

THE MOST EFFICIENT ECONOMIC SYSTEM

The second objective is to establish the most efficient economic system. What we want is the highest possible *real* income (clothing, food, conveniences, and necessities) for everyone. Competitive private enterprise and the free market are the basis of the most efficient system because they most expertly resolve the countless economic conflicts which take place all the time. No individual or group is smart enough to decide the right relationship between the millions of factors which are changing every week and even every day.

COMPLETE SOCIALISM

Under complete socialism it becomes impossible to measure efficiency because, with the market in chains, the government must arbitrarily decide what to produce, how much to produce, as well as guess the costs of production. Instead of responding to the ever-changing evaluations of consumers, production is set according to the eye of the official in power.

Brian Summers, **The Freeman**, January 1977.

Only the free market can accomplish this by permitting the laws of supply and demand to operate through free-pricing. How many electric dynamos shall we make, how many pairs of shoes, how many radios, how much cleaning service, how many hotels? These and countless other questions are decided every day in the give and take of the market. It is the only democratic way of deciding these things, for the only other method is for some autocrat to try to do this job arbitrarily, with the backing of the police power of the State....

SELF-EXPRESSION

The third great virtue of the free enterprise system is that it offers every individual the greatest opportunity for self-expression. Collectivism is the opposite of individualism, and therefore the collectivist society is necessarily stultifying in this regard. The great profusion of works of art and literature in the western world where private capitalism exists is sharply contrasted with the well-known poverty of first-rate creative activity in these fields in communist countries.

Finally, and certainly of great importance, is the fact that life under private capitalism encourages maximum spiritual and aesthetic expression on the part of the individual. He can practice his religious convictions with absolutely no restraint and he can promote any ethical ideas which seem to suit him. Furthermore, he can change his ideas when he wishes. The State cannot stop him....

THE DANGER OF COLLECTIVISM

We hear it said, "It can't happen here." It is hard to imagine the United States without individual freedom. But we need only recall the frightening example of the growth to power of Huey Long to become aware of the danger. This persuasive demagogue used government money and government office to further personal control. He finally became the dominant figure in the southwest and was mentioned as a presidential possibility. Long became a dictator, and in his hands vast, accumulated government power could have been used with frightful effect. And it is clear that there can be other Huey Longs.

The danger of a drift toward collectivism is enhanced by the rapid extension of welfare state measures which lead us step by step in this direction. Those who call themselves liberals today often become uneasy when they realize the conflict that arises between safeguarding human freedom and extending the power of the central government. But in practically all such cases the liberal of today is willing to close his eyes to the threat to freedom in favor of the benefits he thinks will come from the extension of government-managed "welfare" measures. Preservation of human freedom is no longer the first principle of those who today call themselves liberals. It is merely one desirable objective — together with others.

TRADITIONAL LIBERALISM

The *traditional* liberal, on the other hand (often today called a conservative), is guided by the concepts of those who built the foundations of liberalism — ranging from John Locke in the seventeenth century on through to John Stuart Mill, author of the classic *On Liberty*, to Woodrow Wilson in our own time.

John Locke inspired the framers of the American Constitution to establish a government of checks and balances with limited power for the federal government. The first ten Amendments to the Constitution, known as the Bill of Rights, are replete with the phrase "Congress shall pass no law" concerning this or that. Another guiding statement of traditional liberal philosophy is Lord Acton's famous dictum, "All power tends to corrupt; absolute power corrupts absolutely." And the traditional liberal understands the wisdom of de Tocqueville who, visiting the United States early in the nineteenth century, made some astute observations about American life. He pointed out, for instance, that over here people solve many major problems for themselves which in Europe were increasingly loaded on to the State. It was the independence, virility, and individualism of Americans that impressed de Tocqueville in those times, and other traditional liberals since.

Very important, too, among traditional liberal concepts, is the rule that economic and social problems must be solved by the individual, the family, the local community — in that order. Only in case of crisis or provable necessity should the federal government enter the scene. By contrast the new-day liberal tends to think of almost every problem — from juvenile delinquency to the health of each individual — as one which must be solved by the federal government. This is a dangerous road for a freedom-loving people.

Viewpoint

The Vices
of Capitalism

Jack Semmens

Anarchism is the theory that *all* forms of
government are an infringement upon personal
liberty and are therefore undesirable. The
following reading, by Jack Semmens, was taken
from an article appearing in the September,
1975 issue of *The Match*, an anarchist journal.
Semmens believes that capitalism, communism, and socialism are all cut from the same
cloth and thus, are equally intolerable. He
concludes that ''only when the engines of State
and corporate regimentation have been utterly
cast aside, can humankind expect to enjoy the
fruits of prosperity that the free environment of
Anarchy would make possible.''

Consider the following questions while reading:

1. How is capitalism defined?
2. What are the weaknesses of capitalism?
3. What is the alternative to capitalism?

Jack Semmes, ''Evils of Capitalism,'' **The Match**, September 1975, pp. 48-50.

DEFENDERS AND CRITICS

Both the critics and the defenders of capitalism have had occasion to espouse exploitation theories and to relate them to their own attitudes toward the system. Marxists, Communists, Socialists, and variants of these ideologies have made extensive, and frequently accurate, argumentation against the exploitive nature of the capitalistic State. Given the opportunity to deal with this problem, however, none of these statist philosophies and their political manifestations have made any serious efforts at eliminating or even ameliorating the abuses. Leftist regimes of varied type, from military dictatorship to parliamentary democracy, to revolutionary juntas, all have failed miserably by the criterion of exploitation. Rather than ending exploitation, these governments have been satisfied to shuffle around the forms, appoint new managers, and generally to perpetuate the division between management and labor that serves as the focal point for exploitative practices.

On the Right, proponents of capitalism have little to offer in the way of dealing with the problem. Like the leftist statists, the right-wing theoreticians would abolish the evil by mere manipulation of words. In the newspeak of governmentalist propaganda, the enslavement of the working classes is done by definitions. Regimentation of the individual within the machinery of the industrial prison and the inevitable expropriation of the product is defended as either necessary discipline under a revolutionary regime or the survival of the fittest under the capitalist plutocracy....

A DISEASED BRAIN

Within the United States, the burgeoning crises in materials shortages, the financial distortions of inflation and bankruptcy, the growing feelings of futility and doom among the population, are all serving as excuses for further authoritarianism. Now that managers outnumber the managed and the top-heavy superstructure of the capitalist economic system is tottering, liberal academicians are banally pontificating that the ultimate solution lies in one big superbureaucracy, a centralized agency of governmental and corporate hierarchy that will direct all things. Making analogies to biology, authoritarian schemers see the coming of a giant and powerful State that will serve as the central nervous system of the body politic. Overlooked, of course, is the fact that his brain is diseased. Finalization of the pseudo-neural links of this leviathan entity can only insure the death of every cell.

CORPORATE "FAT CATS"

Capitalistic forms of organization in both business and government are infested with a large, nonproductive and frequently counter-productive element. This element, commonly referred to as management or administration, is in reality nothing but a bureaucratic vampire class. These blood-suckers, while producing nothing of value, become obese with their self-arrogated opulence, reserving for themselves the prime cuts of industry. Corporate executives are quick to complain of long hours of overwork, ulcers, heart trouble, and accompanying ills. Naturally, such "sacrifice" is lavishly compensated with generous salaries, kingly expense accounts, and profitable stock options. More likely than not, however, the fatigue and illness suffered by the big wheels of business are the rewards of lives of dissipation. Plush offices remain vacant throughout the working day, as the would-be occupants are out to lunch or on golf courses "wooing" clients. Long nights turn out to be successions of cocktail parties and booze swilling business conventions. Grown fat from the high living, grown flabby from lack of toil, and weakended from excessive indulgence, it is not surprising that corporate officials would have health problems.

TURNING OFF A MACHINE

When the capitalists can't make a profit, they turn off the machines and they turn us off like we were part of the machines. If General Motors can't make enough money, they just lay off 10,000 people, as if they were turning off a machine.

Peter Camejo [Socialist Workers Party candidate for president in 1976], from a speech delivered at the University of Chicago on December 2, 1975.

THE WORKER SUFFERS

Succumbing to the sicknesses spawned by their execrable lifestyle may seem poetic justice. Unfortunately, though, the capitalists are not the only ones to suffer for their abuses. All of society must bear the burdens of the system. Workers must face frustration, as the petty thoughts of the alcohol-besotted brains within corporate management strut about, inflicting the work processes with childish regimentation. Forgetting that the lives and prosperity of all are dependent upon production, business administrators are free to concentrate on such critical matters as the length of employees' hair, style of clothing, social attitudes, and general ass-kissing proclivities. This puerile approach to the tasks of organizing the industrial enterprise is classically illustrated by the vocalized opinions of William Martin, president of the Phillips Petroleum Corporation: ''The worst thing that can happen,'' says Martin, ''is to have an employee that doesn't fit. A corporation has to have regimentation in order to run.'' The uninitiated might have thought that the worst that could happen would be more serious than the nonconformity of some employees. What about safety hazards, production breakdowns, financial blundering, and the like? We have heard of businesses closing down or experiencing serious losses due to fires and floods, faulty machinery, and poor investment decisions. Perusal of the book ''Great Business Disasters'' by Isadore Barmish reveals such debacles as the Edsel, the Penn-Central bank-

ruptcy, Equity Funding, and many more, not one of which could be traced to nonconformity, hair length, or any of the inane considerations so dear to the hearts of top management.

Studies conducted within the organization of a large bank in the state of Arizona disclose, not surprisingly, abysmally poor efficiency. It is not unusual to find departments operating at levels of productivity substantially below 50%. Organizational units are weighed down by top-heavy bureaucracies, stifling chains of command, obstructionist bank policies, and corporate intrigue. Valuable time and energy are consumed in infantile plots, as jealous department chieftains sabotage one another. The contest for sinecures sees organizational charts drawn and redrawn in an endless procession of non-accomplishment....

CANNIBALISM

The rationale for the predatory behavior of the capitalists goes beyond the mere gluttonous predilections of the ruling minority. Capitalism by its very own inner logic leads to cannibalism. In an environment where anything goes in the pursuit of profit, corporate entities that cannot possibly subsist on the nonproduction they engender turn upon one another in an obscene orgy of mutual destruction....

We can see the big eating the small. Finding that even the exploitive theft of labor is inadequate to overcome the losses from mismanagement, business units begin by devouring the middle classes and petty bourgeois. Small savers and investors get the lowest rates of return for the use of their money, while small borrowers must pay the highest rates. Brokerage firms serve as well paid conduits for channeling money from the small investor to the rich....

Unable to compete fairly in a free market environment, the bloated giants of corporate capitalism engage in a never ending struggle to rig the rules in their favor. Using the impeccable logic of the system, namely that everybody's doing it, businesses bargain covertly and overtly with the corrupt politicians and administrators of the governmental apparatus. Bribes in the form of campaign contributions show up in the coffers of politicians of every stripe. The objectives sought by this and other lobbying techniques are legislation, agency rulings, administrative decrees, or whatever that will give the petitioning corporation coercive control over the marketplace. In this manner, monopolies are granted, prices fixed, tariffs imposed, and competition restricted or prohibited....

Only Anarchism offers hope of escape from the nightmare world of the exploiters, parasites, cannibals, and ignoramuses. Only when the engines of State and corporate regimentation have been utterly cast aside, can humankind expect to enjoy the fruits of prosperity that the free environment of Anarchy would make possible. There is no trade-off between liberty and material well-being. The sooner that this statist lie is overcome, the sooner we can begin a new era of advanced civilization.

Viewpoint  13

Capitalism and
Certain Moral Principles

Benjamin A. Rogge

A PhD from Northwestern University, Benjamin
A. Rogge has taught economics at the University of Minnesota, Northwestern University,
and Wabash College. A frequent contributor to
conservative publications, he co-authored the
textbook *Introduction to Economics*. In the
following viewpoint, he attempts to explain why
economic freedom is consistent with ''certain
fundamental moral principles of life itself.''

Consider the following questions while reading:

1. How is capitalism consistent with the moral principles of
   life?
2. What relationship does capitalism have to individual
   freedom?
3. How is economic freedom related to political freedom?

Benjamin A. Rogge, ''The Case for Economic Freedom,'' **The Freeman**, September 1963, pp.
3-12.

THE MORAL ARGUMENT

My central thesis is that *the most important part of the case for economic freedom is not its vaunted efficiency as a system for organizing resources, not its dramatic success in promoting economic growth, but rather its consistency with certain fundamental moral principles of life itself.*

I say, ''the most important part of the case'' for two reasons. First, the significance I attach to those moral principles would lead me to prefer the free enterprise system even if it were demonstrably less efficient than alternative systems, even if it were to produce a *slower* rate of economic growth than systems of central direction and control. Second, the great mass of the people of any country is never really going to understand the purely economic workings of *any* economic system, be it free enterprise or socialism. Hence, most people are going to judge an economic system by its consistency with their moral principles rather than by its purely scientific operating characteristics. If economic freedom survives in the years ahead, it will be only because a majority of the people accept its basic morality. The success of the system in bringing ever higher levels of living will be no more persuasive in the future than it has been in the past.

Let me illustrate: The doctrine of man held in general in nineteenth century America argued that each man was ultimately responsible for what happened to him, for his own salvation, both in the here and now and in the hereafter. Thus, whether a man prospered or failed in economic life was each man's individual responsibility: each man had a right to the rewards for success and, in the same sense, deserved the punishment that came with failure. It followed as well that it is explicitly immoral to use the power of government to take from one man to give to another, to legalize Robin Hood. This doctrine of man found its economic counterpart in the system of free enterprise and, hence, the system of free enterprise was accepted and respected by many who had no real understanding of its subtleties as a technique for organizing resources.

As this doctrine of man was replaced by one (largely reflecting Freudian psychology and sociology) which made of man a helpless victim of his subconscious and his environment —

responsible for neither his successes nor his failures — the free enterprise system came to be rejected by many who still had no real understanding of its actual operating characteristics....

Here, then, are two sections of the case for economic freedom as I would construct it. The first section presents economic freedom as an ultimate end in itself and the second presents it as a means to the preservation of the noneconomic elements in total freedom.

INDIVIDUAL FREEDOM OF CHOICE

The first section of the case is made in the stating of it, if one accepts the fundamental premise:

Major premise: Each man should be free to take whatever *action* he wishes, so long as he does not use force or fraud against another;

Minor premise: All economic behavior is ''action'' as identified above;
Conclusion: Each man should be free to take whatever action he wishes in his economic behavior, so long as he does not use force or fraud against another.

In other words, economic freedom is a part of total freedom; *if freedom is an end in itself, as our society has traditionally asserted it to be, then economic freedom is an end in itself, to be valued for itself alone and not just for its instrumental value in serving other goals.*

THE IDEA OF PROPERTY

I realize that the right to possess the fruits of one's toil is the keystone of society and even of human life. I realize that exchange is implicit in the idea of property, and that restrictions on exchange shake the foundations of our right to own anything.

Frederic Bastiat, **Economic Harmonies**.

If this thesis be accepted, then there must always exist a tremendous presumption against each and every proposal for governmental limitation of economic freedom. What is wrong with a state system of compulsory social security? It denies to the individual his *freedom*, his right to choose what he will do with his own money resources. What is wrong with a governmentally enforced minimum wage? It denies to the employer and the employee their individual freedom, their individual rights to enter into any voluntary relationship not involving force or fraud....

I am no dreamer of empty dreams and I do not expect that the day will ever come when this principle of economic freedom as

Don Hesse © 1977, St. Louis Globe Democrat. Reprinted with permission from the L.A. Times Syndicate.

a part of total freedom will be fully accepted and applied. Yet I am convinced that unless this principle is given some standing, unless at least those who examine proposals for each new regulation of the individual by government look on this loss of freedom as a "cost" of the proposed legislation, the chances of free enterprise surviving are small indeed. The would-be controller can always find reasons why it might seem "expedient" to control the individual; and unless slowed down by some general feeling that it is immoral to do so, he will usually have his way.

NONECONOMIC FREEDOMS

So much for the first section of the case. Now for the second. The major premise here is the same, that is, the premise of the rightness of freedom, Here, though, the concern is with the noneconomic elements in total freedom — with freedom of speech, of religion, of the press, of personal behavior. My thesis is that these freedoms are not likely to be long preserved in a society that has denied economic freedom to its individual numbers....

It is precisely because I believe these noneconomic freedoms to be so important that I believe economic freedom to be so important. The argument here could be drawn from the wisdom of the Bible and the statement that "where a man's treasure is, there will his heart be also." Give me control over a man's economic actions, and hence over his means of survival, and except for a few occasional heroes, I'll promise to deliver to you men who think and write and behave as you want them to.

PARTLY SOCIALIZED

Of course, we are not facing as yet a fully socialized America, but only one in which there is significant government intervention in a still predominantly private enterprise economy. Do these interventions pose any threat to the noneconomic freedoms? I believe they do.

First of all, the total of coercive devices now available to any administration of either party at the national level is so great that true freedom to work actively against the current administration (whatever it might be) is seriously reduced....

Secondly, the form of these interventions is such as to threaten seriously one of the real cornerstones of all freedoms — equality before the law. For example, farmers and trade union members are now encouraged and assisted in doing precisely that for which businessmen are sent to jail (i.e., acting collusively to manipulate prices). The blindfolded Goddess of Justice has been encouraged to peek and she now says, with the jurists of the ancient regime, "First tell me who you are and then I'll tell you what your rights are." A society in which such gross inequalities before the law are encouraged in economic life is not likely to be one which preserves the principle of equality before the law generally.

You may be puzzled, then, that I do not rest my case for economic freedom on its productive achievements; on its buildings, its houses, its automobiles, its bathtubs, its wonder drugs, its television sets, its sirloin steaks and green salads with Roquefort dressings. I neither feel within myself nor do I hear in the testimony of others any evidence that man's search for pupose, his longing for fulfillment, is in any significant way relieved by these accomplishments. I do not scorn these accomplishments nor do I worship them. Nor do I find in the lives of those who do worship them any evidence that they find ultimate peace and justification in their idols.

I rest my case rather on the consistency of the free market with man's essential nature, on the basic morality of its system of rewards and punishments, on the protection it gives to the integrity of the individual.

The free market cannot produce the perfect world, but it can create an environment in which each imperfect man may conduct his lifelong search for purpose in his own way, in which each day he may order his life according to his own imperfect vision of his destiny, suffering both the agonies of his errors and the sweet pleasure of his successes. This freedom is what it means to be a man; this is the God-head, if you wish.

I give you, then, the free market, the economic expression of man's freedom itself and the guarantor of all his other freedoms.

14

"Let's Start Talking About Socialism"

John Buell and Tom DeLuca

The following reading was co-authored by John
Buell, assistant editor of *The Progressive* and
Tom DeLuca, a member of the political science
faculty at Marquette University. The authors
explore some of the contradictions of capitalism
and the failure of liberal reform to remedy
them. Only in a democratic socialist America,
they maintain, will the gross inequities of
capitalism be eliminated.

Consider the following questions while reading:

1. What are the inherent defects of capitalism?
2. How is freedom of speech curtailed under capitalism?
3. Why is socialism offered as an alternative to capitalism?

John Buell and Tom DeLuca, ''Let's Start Talking About socialism,'' **The Progressive**, March
1977, pp. 24-27. Reprinted by permission from **The Progressive**, 408 West Gorham Street,
Madison, Wisconsin 53703. Copyright © 1977 (1975), The Progressive, Inc.

SOCIALISM: "A DIRTY WORD"

Let's start talking about socialism. It has always been a dirty word in America, an "un-American" term we associate with the denial of freedom. Yet ours is the only modern industrialized nation in which socialism does not figure in the political dialogue.

The exclusion of socialism from our politics is a luxury we can no longer afford. We must start talking about socialism because the contradictions of our capitalist system become more obvious every day — and so does the inadequacy of "liberal" reform....Between 1960 and 1969 — the years of the New Frontier and the Great Society — the richest one-fifth of the population increased its share of national income from 43 to 45 per cent. The wealthiest 5 per cent of the population holds 40 per cent of the national wealth, and 1 per cent of the population holds 51 per cent of all corporate stock. Though such disparities are often rationalized on the grounds that capitalism does provide economic growth, the real take-home pay of the average American worker is virtually the same today as it was in 1967.

Reforms of the system have brought neither economic stability nor economic justice. In fact, substantial inequality and cyclical instability are essential attributes of capitalism. Only the promise of profits and high income encourage investment, and an increase in unemployment must be encouraged from time to time to "discipline" the labor force and diminish its demands.

These inherent defects of capitalism are recognized and understood by more Americans than ever before. Several recent public opinion polls have documented profound and pervasive alienation from our corporate system. Yet the socialist alternative remains taboo, Americans associate socialism with the denial of freedom. They know that political dissidents are routinely and brutally repressed in the Soviet Union and the Eastern European nations that call themselves socialist, and they assume — and are constantly encouraged to assume — that if socialism were established in the United States, it would inevitably be accompanied by similar repression....

LIMITED FREEDOM OF SPEECH

Freedom of speech, properly the most sacred of liberal values, exists only precariously in a capitalist economy — especially as a few firms accumulate incredible concentrations of wealth and influence. Money endows capitalists with disproportionate power within the political process — power to buy elections, to hire lobbyists, to shape legislation, and to impede the effects of laws through the courts. Dissident workers can be fired and blacklisted, and when labor becomes too ''militant'' or local government too demanding, the large corporation can simply move its operations to ''a more favorable climate.''

Even the opportunity to develop coherent political perspectives and organize around essential issues is limited by mind-deadening labor, isolation from other workers, and control of the mass media by the power elite. In these circumstances, many workers come to feel that their problems — boredom, for example — are merely personal, reflecting their own inadequacy.

CONVENTIONAL WISDOM OBSOLETE

The conventional wisdom of American reform, which is now forty years old, has become obsolete. A modernized, ameliorated, but still basically capitalist society cannot, even in its welfare state variant, progressively deal with the incredible challenges of the new age that has already begun.
Robert Bellah, ''Coming Around to Socialism,'' **The Nation**, December 28, 1974.

Freedom of thought and speech should never be dismissed by socialists as ''middle-class luxuries.'' They are, in fact, indispensable to any humane society. But under capitalism, the opportunity to exercise fully free speech, like the opportunity to engage in fully rewarding work, is reserved to a fortunate few.

Those who defend capitalism as the bulwark of freedom ignore the problems of everyday life that confront most people in our society. This failure is a consequence not merely of class status but also of certain assumptions about man and society. Capitalists assume that people are "naturally" egoistic and competitive, and that a market economy best expresses and channels these instincts. But people's motives are shaped in important ways by the kind of society in which they live, and there have been many societies which lacked the materialism and egocentricity that characterize ours. We are, after all, instructed all our lives to "get ahead" in school and on the job, and to look to the accumulation of consumer goods as the road to personal fulfillment.

EGOISM AND CRUELTY

Yet the system grudgingly yields some opportunities for co-operative and creative activities. The proliferation of participant sports and do-it-yourself activities shows that there is a human potential for cooperation and creativity — a potential that is usually frustrated by the system. High rates of worker absenteeism, even during the present "recession," are an obvious indicator of profound dissatisfaction with the kind of personal growth our system allows.

Socialists do not claim that people can be angels. They will have moments of egoism and cruelty no matter how society is organized, and there will be conflict and contention. But an individual can reach his highest potential only if social institutions encourage the best instincts — those of which he or she is most proud. These benign impulses are not likely to flourish

when our jobs, our schools, and our culture are designed to foster our capacity to accumulate, to compete, and to dominate. To expect a just and humane society to emerge from such ''realistic'' social structures is truly utopian.

Since socialists assume that human nature emerges from the kind of society in which we live, they argue that the highest freedom is not simply the ability to take one's place on the social ladder, but the opportunity to assume control over and constantly reshape the basic institutions of society. When people own the productive apparatus of society and have abolished the traditional hierarchies of the workplace, they can redesign their jobs, their leisure, their culture, and their politics in more fulfilling ways. This kind of freedom is essential to the creation of a society in which self-development and true community do not contradict but complement each other....

CONTROL BY THE WORKERS

We must admit, that a democratic socialist society cannot guarantee people a higher standard of living as conventionally defined. What it must do is guarantee the democratic determination of how people will live and work — and thereby ensure greater equality and a higher quality of life. In our capitalist economy, the most fundamental decisions — how much we produce, what we produce, how much we consume, what we consume — are made for us by an elite which is always guided by its quest for profits, power, and privilege. Democratic socialism would leave these decisions to the producers themselves.

That kind of society would require not only the protection of political democracy and the public ownership of key industries, but also the achievement of fundamental structural changes for which Western Europe already provides a few examples. In some industries in France, Belgium, and Italy, workers are demanding broader control of the work process. They have created factory-level committees which control training programs, demand access to company books, and redefine jobs. This is more than ''job enrichment,'' which merely dresses up old power relations. The assumption is that all workers should participate in management and should have equally fulfilling jobs, that while specialization may be necessary, its forms can be determined by the workers themselves.

Just as 19th Century liberals saw property as the means by by which to guarantee liberty, Twentieth Century socialists should recognize that liberty is assured only when we control the work process. With more rewarding jobs and fuller control over their workplaces, workers can develop the solidarity, competence, and confidence that can make their formal political freedoms more meaningful.

Since worker control would require some decentralization of political power, ways would have to be found to integrate various economic sectors. The economy would have to be planned nationally as well as locally by associations of workers representing various sectors and regions. The Federal Government could make decisions about how resources would be allocated among such priorities as defense, housing, and health. Regional and local bodies could plan how these resources should best be used to meet local needs. Whenever possible, important decisions would be left to local bodies....

A democratic socialist society would eliminate gross inequalities in wealth as well as work. These two concerns are inseparable. The conservative who suggests that monetary inequality is an essential incentive for work is right — in our society, where the most demeaning jobs will not be performed unless the worker daily confronts the threat of unemployment and financial ruin. When jobs are redesigned and the most tedious or dangerous work is rotated, the incentives for work need not be merely monetary. Income disparities could be reduced, and greater equality in income and work life would protect the individual from economic as well as political and psychological domination. Conflicts of interest and viewpoint would remain, but when the economic security of all is guaranteed, such divisions lose their present brutal nature. Workers, for example, would not have to support a war to protect their jobs. Thus, democratic socialism would raise the level of politics rather than eliminate it....Socialism, properly construed and designed, can significantly enhance the freedom we enjoy. The time has come to begin talking about how to build such a socialism — here in the United States.

Exercise 3

Distinguishing Primary From Secondary Sources

A rational person must always question his or her various sources of information. Scholars, for example, usually distinguish between primary sources (eyewitness accounts) and secondary sources (writings based on primary or eyewitness accounts or other secondary sources). Most textbooks are examples of secondary sources. A diary written by a Civil War veteran about the Civil War is one example of a primary source. In order to be a critical reader, one must be able to recognize primary sources. This, however, is not enough. Eyewitness accounts do not always provide accurate descriptions. Historians may find ten different eyewitness accounts that each interpret an event differently; they must then decide which of these accounts provide the most objective and accurate interpretations. In addition, primary sources are not always better than secondary sources. Frequently, secondary sources will prove accurate while primary sources can be unreliable.

Test your skill in evaluating sources by participating in the following exercise. Pretend you are living 1000 years in the future. Your teacher tells you to write an essay about the causes of political conflict between the U.S. and Cuba between 1960 and 1975. First, consider carefully each of the following sources and locate the primary (eyewitness) accounts. Second, rank all sources by assigning the number (1) to the source you think might be the most objective and accurate, and so on until the ranking is finished. See if you can find any secondary sources that might be better than a primary source.

Since most sources cited below are fictitious, you cannot read them and judge their accuracy. You will, however, recognize some of the people mentioned. You must guess about how their frames of reference and political views might have influenced their perceptions of U.S.-Cuba relations. The activity is designed to help you begin exploring the kind of source analysis needed for intelligent and rational thinking about social issues. Assume that all of the following sources deal with the broad problem of political conflict between the U.S. and Cuba from 1960 to 1975. Discuss and compare your source evaluations with those of other class members.

_____ 1. A magazine article written in 1970 by President Nixon.

_____ 2. The diary of a conservative French journalist who had lived in Cuba between 1960 and 1970. He was reporting on events in Cuba for a French paper.

_____ 3. A senate speech in 1968 by Edward Kennedy, a leading liberal senator from Massachusetts.

_____ 4. A speech in 1958 by the National Commander of the American Legion.

_____ 5. A news film discovered in the year 2000 A.D. The film covered a 1965 interview with President Johnson.

_____ 6. A book written in 1969 by an American professor of political science who was a professed marxist.

_____ 7. A taped interview in the year 2164 with the leader of the National Organization for Women.

_____ 8. A speech in 1968 by Barry Goldwater, a leading conservative senator from Arizona.

_____ 9. The tape of a Cuban T.V. interview with Fidel Castro discovered in the year 2525 A.D. The interview was made in 1983.

_____ 10. A book written in 1966 by a communist Chinese historian. He had never visited Cuba or the U.S.

Chapter 4

Capitalism

The Future
of Capitalism?

INTRODUCTION

Ever since capitalism became the dominant economic system in western Europe, critics have been predicting its downfall. In the last century, Karl Marx wrote that within itself capitalism possessed ''the seeds of its own destruction.'' In this century, Nikita Khrushchev said ''we will bury you,'' implying the ultimate demise of the capitalistic system at the hands of international communism. Even many who support the system see an imminent danger of its crumbling under its own weight in the absence of immediate basic reforms.

The next series of viewpoints deal with the problem of capitalism's future. While reading them, it might be useful to consider the following questions. Is the capitalistic system answering the economic needs of society today, or should it be reformed? Is capitalism beyond reform and thus in need of replacing? Would it be possible to develop a compromise system containing the most favorable elements of capitalism and an alternative system?

Viewpoint  15

Capitalism
Will Prosper

Time **Magazine Feature Article**

When Karl Marx wrote his *Manifesto of the Communist Party* in 1847, he expressed the conviction that capitalism was in its final days. He was certain that the international labor movement, conscious of its importance and united strength, soon would lead the revolt to overthrow the bourgeoisie and its lackeys. Capitalism would be replaced by a world communist state shorn of national boundaries and collectively governed by the proletariat. The following reading attempts to show why Marx was wrong in 1847 and why capitalism will not be replaced (at least in the foreseeable future) by communism or any other collective economic system.

Consider the following questions while reading:

1. What role does the profit motive play in capitalism?
2. How does history support capitalism?
3. Why is capitalism better at meeting human needs than other methods of government?

''Can Capitalism Survive?'' **Time**, July 14, 1975, pp. 63. Reprinted by permission from TIME, The Weekly Newsmagazine; copyright Time Inc. 1975.

THE PROFIT MOTIVE

One of the capitalist market system's enduring strengths is...
its reliance on the profit motive which, like it or not, is a powerful human drive. To many idealists the primacy of the profit
motive has long seemed to be a sanctification of selfishness
that produces a brutalizing, beggar-thy-neighbor society. Vic-
torian Moralist John Ruskin denounced "the deliberate blasphemy of Adam Smith: Thou shalt hate the Lord thy God, damn
His laws, and covet thy neighbour's goods."

But capitalism has the overwhelmingly powerful defense of
simple realism. There *is* just enough of a "Scotchman" in most
people to make them work harder for their own advancement
than for the good of their fellows — a fact that regularly embar-
rasses socialist regimes. The Soviet Union permits collective
farmers to cultivate small private plots in their spare time and
sell the produce for their own profit. Those plots account for a
mere 4% of the land under cultivation in the U.S.S.R. — yet,
by value, they produce a fourth of the country's food.

Profits and other incentives are indispensable to any economic
progress. A product or service that is sold for exactly the cost of
producing it yields no margin to raise wages, buy new
machinery or pursue research leading to new products. Only
profits can finance that — whether in a capitalist or a socialist
society.

TWO BASIC QUESTIONS

The argument between capitalism and authoritarian economic
systems comes down to two questions: Which system can make
the most efficient use of manpower, materials and money to
create the greatest opportunties for free choice, personal
development and material well-being for the greatest number
of people? And which system is more just and satisfying in
human terms?

An authoritarian economy appeals to many human instincts. It
offers stability and security at the expense of freedom and a
greater degree of economic (though not political) equality than
capitalism. It can provide full employment by creating a surfeit
of make-work, low-productivity (and thus low-paying) jobs. It
keeps prices stable by fixing them, almost invariably at high

levels in terms of real income. Yet even the meanness of living standards in such a system may have a certain attraction for millions of people outside those countries who are repelled or surfeited by commercial values. Distrust of money lies deep in the West's history, from St. Francis of Assisi and the Anabaptists to the modern romantics. Authoritarian economies are as materialistic as capitalism, if not more so, but they are often perceived differently. And the ability of the command economy to centralize power has an irresistible appeal for otherwise shaky leaders of developing nations. As Moynihan observes, many of the developing nations have an ''interest in deprecating the economic achievements of capitalism, since none of their own managed economies are doing well.''

HISTORY SUPPORTS CAPITALISM

On the historical record, capitalism clearly is more enriching — in every major way. Capitalism, says Eckstein, ''is the only engine that has been developed so far that encourages people to be highly innovative, to develop new products and processes.'' Profit-seeking capitalists have developed all the vital machines of ''post-industrial'' society. In contrast, centrally managed economies have rarely done well at developing civilian high-technology industry — largely because inventors lack incentive. In socialist economics the same lack has led to appalling shoddiness in many of the services that provide life's amenities.

ADMIRATION FOR THE MARKETPLACE

Not all intellectuals are critics of capitalism. Much of the new empirical work in economics actually supports the market position. Among economists I see a growing respect for the market. If you want to know where there is great admiration for the market place, go to the economists and intellectuals of Eastern Europe, where they have tried to do without markets!

Benjamin A. Rogge, **Vital Speeches**, July 1, 1974.

Capitalists also have produced a far greater quantity and variety of consumer goods and services than socialist central planners. The reason: for all its weaknesses, the market functions as a superbly adaptive super-computer that continuously monitors consumer tastes. Says Walter Heller: "The private market makes trillions of decisions without any central regulation. It is a fantastic cybernetic device that processes huge amounts of information in the form of the consumer voting with his dollars, the retailer telegraphing back to the wholesaler, the wholesaler to the producer."

COMMUNISM BORROWS FROM CAPITALISM

Communist nations have paid the market the ultimate compliment by trying to introduce elements of market pricing into their own economies, so far with meager success. The trademarks of Communist economies remain indelible: low productivity, shortages of goods, lengthy queues in stores, yearslong waits for apartments. In order to spur initiative, most Communist countries also have huge and growing differences in real income (and perquisites) between commissar and collective farmer. Nikita Khrushchev once replied to a charge that the Soviet Union was going capitalist: "Call it what you will, incentives are the only way to make people work harder."

More important, capitalism's superior productivity is not solely a matter of electric toothbrushes and throwaway soft-drink bottles: the system also does better at filling basic human needs like food. Farmers in the capitalist U.S., Canada and Australia grow enough not only to feed their own peoples but also to export huge surpluses. In contrast, the Soviet Union — although 30% of its workers labor on its vast farmlands — has to import food. So does India, which permits private farming but insists out of socialist principle that the produce be sold at unrealistically low prices.

FREEDOM ABOVE ALL

The freedom of capitalist society at its best must be prized above all. True, some dictatorships are capitalist because most of the economy is privately owned. Still, the major capitalist nations all have popularly elected governments that guard the right of free speech and assembly. Capitalism demands, by definition, that the individual be free within broad limits to spend and invest his money any way he pleases, to own private property and to enter any business or profession that attracts him. The state that grants those significant freedoms demonstrates a reluctance to interfere in the citizen's daily life.

In sharp contrast, the managed economies exist mostly in one-party states or under completely totalitarian regimes. Any government that tries to dictate almost every decision on production, prices and wages assumes an arbitrary power that would be impossible to reconcile with political freedom. In most managed economies, for example, a strike by workers is a crime against the state; it can hardly be prohibited without suppressing the right to advocate such a strike.

In sum, there is no alternative to capitalism that credibly promises both wealth and liberty. Despite its transitory woes and weaknesses, capitalism in the foreseeable future will not only survive but also stands to prosper and spread. Perhaps the most balanced judgment of Adam Smith's wondrous system is Winston Churchill's famous conclusion about democracy: It is the worst system — except for all those other systems that have been tried and failed.

Capitalism
Will Die

Sidney Lens

A native of Newark, New Jersey, Sidney Lens
has been active in the labor movement since the
1950s. Lens is a lecturer at the University of
Chicago and a member of the board of directors
of the Chicago Council on Foreign Relations. A
long-time advocate of international socialism,
he has written extensively on the subject. His
published works include: *The Counterfeit
Revolution*, *The Crisis of American Labor*, *A
World in Revolution*, and *The Day Before
Doomsday*. In the reading below, he explains
why capitalism is a "terminally ill patient" and
suggests that it be replaced by a political-
economic system which is at once socialist and
internationalist.

Consider the following questions while reading:

1. Why is capitalism sick?
2. What do debt and militarism have to do with capitalism?
3. How does the author distinguish between private and public
   socialism?
4. What alternative to capitalism does Lens suggest?

Sidney Lens, "Capitalism's Last Gap," **Skeptic**, May-June 1977, pp. 14-17, 52, 53. Condensed
from issue #19 of Skeptic Magazine and reprinted by permission. © 1977 Skeptic Magazine Inc.
All rights reserved.

When a terminally ill patient has cheated death four times, he (or his doctor) is likely to become overconfident the fifth time he gets sick.

The fact is that capitalism has been kept alive by artifical means for two generations and has two potentially terminal ailments — debt and militarism....

THE DEATH WATCH

Are we in the throes of our last illness? The standard reaction is to brush such a question aside: "We've had problems before and we've solved them. Solutions will always be found." Maybe so. Some of the difficulties no doubt will be overcome — the economy, for instance, may gain momentum for a time — but if we trace the present symptoms to their historical antecedents, optimism yields to doubt. The record shows that whatever prosperity capitalism has enjoyed since 1933 has been synthetic, bought by *debt* and *militarism*. The strange anomaly of present-day capitalism is that while it cannot survive *without* debt and militarism, it can no longer survive *with* them either.

Let's see why.

"In 1932," Harry Truman later observed, "the private enterprise system was close to collapse. There was real danger that the American people" (and people elsewhere) "might turn to some other system."

How did the "free enterprise" system revive? Actually, it didn't. It was jettisoned and supplanted by "controlled capitalism," then "state-managed capitalism" — or what might properly be called "private socialism." Adam Smith and his theories about the self-regulating character of the "free market" were shown the door; John Maynard Keynes was invited in to explain the magic of "compensatory spending" and "deficit financing." Franklin Roosevelt didn't like Keynes, but he practiced the Keynesian magic. So did Adolf Hitler.

Under the Keynesian doctrine, the state — which Adam Smith had insisted must leave the free market to its own devices (*laissez-faire*) — intervened to do for capitalists and their system what they couldn't do for themselves. It compensated

99

for the decrease in investments by disbursing investment money from the government till, and it compensated for the decrease in purchasing power by forcing employers to pay higher wages and by doling out welfare, unemployment compensation, pay for make-work, and Social Security. It established, in effect, two welfare states, one for business to keep it from drowning, another for the lower classes to keep them from entertaining thoughts of revolution.

KEYNES AND THE NEW DEAL

The New Deal of course didn't have the money to prime pumps and pay for relief, so the government went into debt — $3-4 billion a year. Keynes called this ''deficit financing,'' the corollary to ''compensatory spending.'' When cynics asked who was going to make good the debts, they were told (a) we would begin repayment when times got better; and (b) it didn't matter anyway because ''we owe the money to ourselves.''

Why didn't it occur to Keynes and Roosevelt to place the major corporations in government hands — to detach the respirator, so to speak? Adam Smith's ''free enterprise'' was obviously bankrupt. If government were the only force that could save it, why shouldn't government take it over and run it for society's benefit? Why should it reward business for inefficiency and ineptness?

MONOPOLY CAPITAL

We in the United States can relieve monopoly capital of its crisis of ''purpose'' by fundamentally changing the purpose of our economic and governmental structure to serve the interests of the people's welfare. This, of course, in general terms, spells socialism.

Gus Hall, **World Magazine**, September 6, 1975.

Roosevelt *did* save capitalism in the US (and Hitler saved it in Germany, as did Chamberlain in Britain, Daladier in France). FDR saved it but didn't make it robust. For despite all of the New Deal ministrations, unemployment by 1939 had dropped by only 3.5 million; more than 20 percent of the labor force remained jobless. It was World War II that put them to work, and the Cold War (plus small hot wars in Korea and Vietnam) that kept them working thereafter. The only compensatory spending that seems to have been effective was the $160 billion spent on World War II and the $1.75 trillion spent later to maintain the greatest military machine in history. Meanwhile the national debt grew from $43 billion in 1940 to $257.4 billion in 1950, to $288.3 billion in 1970, to $620.3 billion in 1976.

To speak in less statistical terms, we mortgaged the earnings of our children, grandchildren and great-grandchildren to pay for our own comfort now....

THE THREAT OF COMMUNISM

Washington welded militarism to economic aid. Allies were to be covered by an American military umbrella. Governments tied to the ''American system'' were given weapons and

WHICH: CONTROLS OR NO CONTROLS?

military training to defend themselves against their own people. To back up this system of world control, the Pentagon had to be ensconced in bases around the world (2,500 major and minor ones).

Hence, the United States fashioned a great armada of warships, planes and tanks and an arsenal of 30,000 nuclear bombs (capable of killing everyone on earth 12 times) to defend a new form of imperialism. It could not do otherwise, given its capitalist imperatives, for if it didn't offer to defend and aid various countries they would seek help elsewhere, in some cases from the Soviet Union, thus cutting off the United States from vital markets.

For a quarter of a century this system worked. One might ruminate that writing checks against the future and provoking a runaway arms race was a cockeyed way to run the store, but living standards were never higher, so who cared?

But now, the whole edifice is crumbling because the monumental budget deficits and balance of payments deficits that financed foreign aid, the arms race and ''private socialism'' were too great even for the American colossus to carry. They finally undermined the cornerstone of modern capitalism, the dollar....

THE END OF THE LINE

We have come, it seems, to the end of a long journey. Only the vast resources of the United States saved capitalism after the Russian Revolution and then again, during and after World War II. Now the bastion of capitalism itself has been seriously weakened.

For 40-odd years the US followed a policy of *socializing losses* or undertaking for business what business couldn't undertake for itself. Since US shipowners were uncompetitive with foreign shipowners, government paid a subsidy of a certain amount each year for every seafaring job. Since shipbuilders were uncompetitive it paid a subsidy for American-built ships. It spent tens of billions to build factories during World War II because business wouldn't or couldn't do it. It allocated tens of billions for research and development ($15 billion a year or more today). It subsidized the defense industry, aviation, exports and imports (through the Ex-Im Bank), petroleum (through tax breaks) and indirectly the automobile industry (through its road-building program) and construction (through a host of tax incentives). It guaranteed tens of billions in business loans, billions in foreign investments overseas and, in the case of passenger railroad services, nationalized an industry that was losing money to assure it a subsequent profit (from the coffers of Amtrak, which pays the railroads on a cost-plus basis).

Private socialism, however, has reached its outer limits. More than a third of the gross national product today is generated by government (and in Britain, 52 percent). Burdened with debt and inflation, Washington now has to retrench; America's cities and educational systems, beginning with New York, are retrenching even more...

The portents are ominous. Nevertheless, solutions to society's problems are available. The imperative is that capitalist anarchy be replaced by planning, that capitalist greed ("profit maximization") yield to social concern, and that national sovereignty be abandoned in favor of worldwide integration. We can no longer choose between capitalism and socialism; the choice is between an inept *private* socialism and a socialism that is both public and internationalist.

Viewpoint 17

Looking Backward: A Time for Change

Milton Friedman

Milton Friedman is one of the leading and most influential defenders of traditional capitalism in the United States today. A winner of the Nobel Prize for economics in 1976, he has held several academic and government positions, including Professor of Economics at the University of Chicago and Principal Economist, Division of Tax Research, United States Treasury Department. Friedman has authored several books, the most widely read being *Capitalism and Freedom* published in 1962. The following is an excerpt from a speech delivered at Pepperdine University, Los Angeles, on February 9, 1977. While admitting that the future of the free enterprise system is uncertain, Friedman explains why he believes that it may ultimately prevail.

Consider the following questions while reading:

1. Why does movement toward a collectivist society threaten freedom?
2. How is free enterprise defined?
3. Why has the growth of government come about?
4. What alternative does the author suggest?

Milton Friedman, ''The Future of Capitalism,'' **Vital Speeches**, March 15, 1977, pp. 333, 335-37. Reprinted with permission.

My subject is "The Future of Capitalism." When I speak of the future of capitalism I mean the future of competitive capitalism — a free enterprise capitalism. In a certain sense, every major society is capitalistic. Russia has a great deal of capital but the capital is under the control of governmental officials who are supposedly acting as the agents of the state. That turns capitalism (state capitalism) into a wholly different system than a system under which capital is controlled by individuals in their private capacity as owners and operators of industry. What I want to speak about tonight is the future of private enterprise — of competitive capitalism.

The future of private enterprise capitalism is also the future of a free society. There is no possibility of having a politically free society unless the major part of its economic resources are operated under a capitalistic private enterprise system.

THE TREND TOWARD COLLECTIVISM

The real question therefore is the future of human freedom. The question that I want to talk about is whether or not we are going to complete the movement that has been going on for the past forty or fifty years, away from a free society and toward a collectivist society. Are we going to continue down the path until we have followed Chile by losing our political freedom and coming under the thumb of an all-powerful government? Or are we going to be able to halt that trend, perhaps even reverse it, and establish a greater degree of freedom?

One thing is clear, we cannot continue along the lines that we have been moving. In 1928, less than fifty years ago, government at all levels — federal, state, and local — spent less than 10 percent of the national income. Two-thirds of that was at the state and local level. Federal spending amounted to less than 3 percent of the national income. Today, total government spending at all levels amounts to 40 percent of the national income, and two-thirds of that is at the federal level. So federal government spending has moved in less than fifty years from 3 percent to over 25 percent — total government spending from 10 percent to 40 percent. Now, I guarantee you one thing. In the next fifty years government spending cannot move from 40 percent of the national income to 160 percent. (Legislatures have tried to legislate that the value of π shall be exactly three and a seventh but they cannot repeal the laws of arithmetic!)

We cannot continue on this path. The question is, will we keep trying to continue on this path until we have lost our freedom and turned our lives over to an all-powerful government in Washington, or will we stop?

In judging this possibility, it's worth talking a little bit about where we are and how we got here — about the present and the past. Let me say at the outset that with all the problems I am going to talk about, this still remains a predominantly free society. There is no great country in the world (there are some small enclaves, but no great country) that offers as much freedom to the individual as the United States does. But having said that we ought also to recognize how far we have gone away from the ideal of freedom and the extent to which our lives are restricted by governmental enactments.

THE FREE ENTERPRISE SYSTEM

In talking about freedom it is important at the outset to distinguish two different meanings on the economic level, of the concept of free enterprise, for there is no term which is more misused or misunderstood. The one meaning that is often attached to free enterprise is the meaning that enterprises shall be free to do what they want. That is not the meaning that has historically been attached to free enterprise. What we really mean by free enterprise is the freedom of individuals to set up enterprises. It is the freedom of an individual to engage in an activity so long as he uses only voluntary methods of getting other individuals to cooperate with him. If you want to see how far we have moved from the basic concept of free enterprise, you can consider how free anyone is to set up an enterprise. You are *not* free to establish a bank or to go into the taxicab business unless you can get a certificate of convenience and necessity from the local, state, or federal authorities. You cannot become a lawyer or a physician or a plumber or a mortician (and you can name many other cases) unless you can get a license from the government to engage in that activity. You cannot go into the business of delivering the mail or providing electricity or of providing telephone service unless you get a permit from the government to do so. You cannot raise funds on the capital market and get other people to lend you money unless you go through the S.E.C. and fill out the 400 pages of forms that they require. To take the latest restriction on freedom, you cannot any longer engage in voluntary deals with others or make bets with other people about the future prices of commodities unless you get the approval of the government....

THE 19TH CENTURY

The closest approach to free enterprise we have ever had in the United States was in the 19th Century. Yet you and your children will hear over and over again in their schools and in their classes the myths that that was a terrible period when the robber barons were grinding the poor miserable people under their heels. That's a myth constructed out of whole cloth. The plain fact is that never in human history has there been a period when the ordinary man improved his condition and benefited his life as much as he did during that period of the 19th Century when we had the closest approach to free enterprise that we have ever had. Most of us in this room, I venture to say, are beneficiaries of that period. I speak of myself. My parents came to this country in the 1890's. Like millions of others they came with empty hands. They were able to find a place in this country, to build a life for themselves and to provide a basis on which their children and their children's children could have a better life. There is no saga in history remotely comparable to the saga of the United States during that era, welcoming millions and millions of people from all over the world and enabling them to find a place for themselves and to improve their lives. And it was possible only because there was an essentially free society.

If the laws and regulations that today hamstring industry and commerce had been in effect in the 19th Century our standard of living today would be below that of the 19th Century. It would have been impossible to have absorbed the millions of people who came to this country.

WHY REGIMENTATION?

What produced the shift? Why did we move from a situation in which we had an essentially free society to a situation of increasing regimentation by government? In my opinion, the fundamental cause of most government intervention is an

Milton Friedman accepting the Nobel Prize for economics.

United Press International, Inc.

unholy coalition between well-meaning people seeking to do good on the one hand, and special interests (meaning you and me) on the other, taking advantage of those activities for our own purposes.

The great movement toward government has not come about as a result of people with evil intentions trying to do evil. The great growth of government has come about because of good people trying to do good. But the method by which they have tried to do good has been basically flawed. They have tried to do good with other people's money. Doing good with other people's money has two basic flaws. In the first place, you never spend anybody else's money as carefully as you spend your own. So a large fraction of that money is inevitably wasted. In the second place, and equally important, you cannot do good with other people's money unless you first get the money away from them. So that force — sending a policeman to take the money from somebody's pocket — is fundamentally at the basis of the philosophy of the welfare state. That is why the attempt by good people to do good has led to disastrous results. It was this movement toward welfare statism that produced the phenomenon in Chile which ended the Allende regime. It is this tendency to try to do good with other people's money that has brought Great Britain — once the greatest nation of the earth, the nation which is the source of our traditions and our values and our beliefs in a free society — to the edge of catastrophe. It will be touch and go whether over the next five years Great Britain will be able to maintain a free society or relapse into collectivism.

When you start on the road to do good with other people's money, it is easy at first. You've got a lot of people to pay taxes and a small number of people with whom you are trying to do good. But the later stages become harder and harder. As the number of people on the receiving end grows, you end up in the position where you are taxing 50 percent of the people to help 50 percent of the people. Or, really, 100 percent of the people to distribute benefits to 100 percent! The *reductio ad absurdum* of this policy is a proposal to send out a rain of $50.00 checks to all and sundry in the next few months....

TWO POSSIBLE SCENARIOS
Where shall we go from here? There are two possible scen-

arios. The one (and I very much fear it's the more likely) is that we will continue in the direction in which we have been going, with gradual increases in the scope of government and government control. If we do continue in that direction, two results are inevitable. One result is financial crisis and the other is a loss of freedom.

The example of England is a frightening example to contemplate. England has been moving in this direction. We're about twenty years behind England in this motion. But England was moving in this direction earlier than we were moving and has moved much farther. The effects are patent and clear. But at least when England moved in this direction and thus lost its power politically and internationally, the United States was there to take over the defense of the free world. But I ask you, when the United States follows that direction, who is going to take over from us? That's one scenario, and I very much fear it's the more likely one.

The other scenario is that we will, in fact, halt this trend — that we will call a halt to the apparently increasing growth of government, set a limit and hold it back.

There are many favorable signs from this point of view. I may say that the greatest reason for hope, in my opinion, is the inefficiency of government. Many people complain about government waste. I welcome it. I welcome it for two reasons. In the first place, efficiency is not a desirable thing if somebody is doing a bad thing. A great teacher of mine, a mathematical economist, once wrote an article on the teaching of statistics. He said, ''Pedagogical ability is a vice rather than a virtue if it is devoted to teaching error.'' That's a fundamental principle. Government is doing things that we don't want it to do, so the more money it wastes the better.

In the second place, waste brings home to the public at large the fact that government is not an efficient and effective instrument for achieving its objectives. One of the great causes for hope is a growing disillusionment around the country with the idea that government is the all-wise, all-powerful big brother who can solve every problem that comes along, that if only you throw enough money at a problem it will be resolved.

Viewpoint ▨ **18**

Looking Ahead:
A Time for Change

Sam Love

A consultant and writer on energy and environmental issues, Sam Love formerly served as
Coordinator of Environmental Action in
Washington, D.C. In the following reading,
Love asserts that modern industrial society is
afflicted by the "terminal disease of bigness."
While he does not recommend a total dismem-
berment of the existing structure, he does
advocate a massive reorganization of America's
economic system under new, rational lines.

Consider the following questions while reading:

1. What are the signs of capitalism's structural weakness?
2. Why is bigness a disease of industrial society?
3. Why should we let capitalism die?
4. What should take the place of capitalism?

Sam Love, "Let the Old Order Die," **The Progressive**, November 1975, pp. 38-41. Reprinted by
permission from **The Progressive**, 408 West Gorham Street, Madison, Wisconsin 53703. Copyright © 1977 (1975), The Progressive, Inc.

BASIC STRUCTURAL WEAKNESS

Against the economic background of the last few years, it would be a tragic mistake for the American people to be misled by the apparent direction of the aggregate indicators used to assess the official condition of the economy. We are surrounded by signs of basic, structural weakness, among them:

* the recent financial collapse of the railroads,
* some of the largest bank failures since the depression,
* the virtual bankruptcy of New York City,
* the acute distress of various airlines and aerospace corporations,
* drastic sales reductions in the largest industries — home building and automobiles, and
* alarming increases in the price of such basic necessities as food and energy....

MORE ENERGY WILL IMPROVE SOCIETY

Our civilization is a product of our ability to harness and use massive amounts of energy. More specifically, our economic system — capitalism — depends on the high productivity which energy makes possible. Adam Smith, the father of capitalism, observed that such a system could exist because machines "facilitate and abridge labor, and enable one man to do the work of many."

While the harnessing of more concentrated forms of energy may initially increase jobs and social wealth, we have reached a stage that permits one person to do the work which previously required hundreds. Most economists and corporate executives tend to cite the positive contribution of such mechanization to the gross national product, but there is a negative side: Machines can displace people. The number of workers who have been displaced by increased use of energy is not easily quantifiable, but some knowledgeable observers estimate that each productive worker is now doing the work that once required 350 laborers....

The abundant energy myth also fails to take into account the fact that energy cannot be utilized without exacting some environmental toll. The price for increased energy use is more stripmining, radioactive waste, air and water pollution, and aesthetic offense. These can hardly be considered social benefits.

BIG IS BEST

Industrial society is afflicted with the terminal disease of bigness. Size has been equated with success for so long that dinosaur-like institutions dominate almost all aspects of our lives. Business leaders may complain about decreases in productivity because of high rates of absenteeism, but it is impossible for workers to feel a part of the massive corporations which dominate production.

As institutions increase in size, they lose flexibility. A prime example is the auto industry's inability to shift away from the internal combustion engine toward such technically feasible alternatives as the turbine or steam engine.

The economies of scale and market manipulation that are facilitated by large units may offer short-term benefits on quarterly report balance sheets, but socially, bigness can result in instability. Again, consider the auto industry: One American in six reportedly earns his or her livelihood as a direct result of the automobile. With such social imbalance, it is little wonder that what's bad for General Motors is bad for the entire economy....

STANDARDIZATION PAYS

A basic tenet of industrial capitalism is the notion that standardization can produce economies of scale, but it also has its pitfalls. For example, nuclear power plants are now being standardized to speed up licensing and achieve economies in production. The process may get reactors on line faster, but when a problem develops with one nuclear plant, it could result in the shutting down of all plants of that type, thus taking a steep toll on electrical production. Such a situation is not hypothetical: In 1974, similar cracks developed in the cooling system of three boiling-water reactors, and twenty-one of the fifty operating reactors were ordered shut down for inspection and repair. Such disruptions cannot occur without affecting the economy....

With such myths underlying public and private decision making, it is little wonder we are in trouble. Decision makers are not confronting the reality that the economy of the United States, as presently structured, is anti-people and anti-nature. It functions relatively smoothly for the interests of big capital, and brutally for the rest of us. Public policymakers must come to accept the fact that the old order is doing its best to die, and that we should let it.

CORPORATE EUTHANASIA

The corporations and banks that are in trouble should be allowed to go under. But while this is happening, social policies must be developed to ease the suffering that will inevitably result from the collapse of the old institutions. The official policy in Congress and statehouses should be *corporate euthanasia*, coupled with programs that make the death of the institutions as painless as possible for the people victimized by their fall — not only workers who may need relocation and re-training, but also small shareholders and retirees who have based their income on stock-based pension plans. By designing such short-term policies as massive public works programs with a recognition that tomorrow will be different, we can channel the social dislocation resulting from the downfall of the large economic structures into constructive directions to help create a viable future society....

CAPITALISM HAS OUTGROWN THE INDIVIDUAL

Capitalism is not what it used to be. It has outgrown the individual. It is possible that it also has outgrown both management and the labor leader. If these things are so, the day may have arrived for a new sort of pioneering in this country: state-control of the economy.

Watson Gordon, **Saturday Review**, June 8, 1957.

Our society needs too much productive work simply to unleash a public works army of leaf rakers for the sake of fighting unemployment. Public works can be creative. Solar collectors can be built, mass transit systems can be constructed, cities can be decentralized, fertility can be restored to the soil, durable houses can be erected, and strip mine scars can be reclaimed.

THE CHOICE IS OURS

We have a choice: We can patch up private corporations with infusions of public capital through Reconstruction Finance Corporation schemes, or we can build a cooperative, people-oriented future. For the amount the Government is now prepared to spend on subsidizing some corporations, the public could purchase a controlling interest. The state of New York could have bought virtually all of the outstanding common stock in Consolidated Edison for the amount it agreed to pay for two of the utility's unfinished power plants last year. With many airlines, railroads, and other corporate interests now requesting subsidies from Congress, an opportunity exists to obtain public control by simply buying up outstanding stock. At that point, serious discussion could begin of ways to reorganize corporations into a new, non-capitalist form. Nationalization, while it may be the best course for such industries as oil and airlines, is not the only public ownership model open to us. Wherever possible, the ''big is best'' myth should be discarded in favor of the ''small is beautiful'' ideal. Utilities and many manufacturing concerns should and could be locally owned and controlled. A pluralistic economic system can combine private corporations, Government-owned corporations, and community-owned cooperatives.

Reorganizing ailing business structures is only part of the task. For our ailing cities, we need Government policies that facilitate decentralization. Small towns and medium size cities can be made more attractive places to live. Small farms can be helped to survive.

We should not allow ourselves to be deterred by the fact that our alternative vision has not been worked out to the final detail. Such times as ours are chaotic and confusing, but they provide immense challenges and opportunities. The ideals of the French Revolution were nurtured in a period not unlike the present. The old feudalist monarchy could no longer serve. Masses of people were dislocated. Food shortages gripped the cities, while the farmers' fields lay fallow. Many thought the end of civilization was at hand. Yet civilization did not end, and positive changes grew out of the seeming chaos. We may well have a similar chance.

Cause and Effect Relationships

This discussion exercise provides practice in the skill of analyzing cause and effect relationships. Causes of human conflict and social problems are usually very complex. The following statements indicate possible causes for urban unrest and conflict. Rank them by assigning the number (1) to the most important cause, number (2) to the second most important, and so on until the ranking is finished. Omit any statements you feel are not causative factors. Add any causes you think have been left out. Then discuss and compare your decisions with those of other class members.

_____ a. Segregated public schools

_____ b. The international communist conspiracy

_____ c. Poverty

_____ d. Unemployment

_____ e. Failure of politicians to pass laws that would fund urban renewal programs

_____ f. Failure of politicians to pass laws that would establish government jobs for the unemployed

_____ g. The tendency of the federal government to meddle too much in the affairs of the city and local governments

_____ h. Lazy people who do not want to work

_____ i. The failure of capitalism to provide jobs for all and a fair distribution of the wealth

117

_____ j. Too many socialist programs like welfare

_____ k. Racial discrimination in all social institutions

_____ l. The tendency for our economic system to operate on the bases of greed and profit rather than concern for the welfare of the individual

_____ m. Other causes you can think of

Selected Bibliography

SMITH AND MARX

Frederick Bender   *The Betrayal of Marx*. New York: Harper and Row, 1975.

Maurice H. Dobb   *On Marxism Today*. London: Leonard and Virginia Woolf at the Hogarth Press, 1932.

Arthur Jenkins   *Adam Smith Today: An Inquiry Into the Nature and Causes of the Wealth of Nations*. New York: R. R. Smith, 1948.

J. Ralph Lindgren   *The Early Writings of Adam Smith*. New York: A. M. Kelley, 1967.

Karl Marx   *Capital: A Critical Analysis of Capitalist Production*. Moscow: Progress Publishers, 1965-1967.

Karl Marx and Frederick Engels   *The Civil War in the United States*. New York: International Publishers, 1969.

Karl Marx and Frederick Engels   *The Communist Manifesto*. New York: Labor News Co., 1948.

Karl Marx   *On Society and Social Change*. Chicago: University of Chicago Press, 1973.

E. Ragston Pike   *Adam Smith: Founder of the Science of Economics*. London: Weidenfeld and Nicolson, 1965.

Hubert Schneider   *Adam Smith's Moral and Political Philosophy*. New York: Hafner Publishing Co., 1948.

Pat Sloan   *Marx and the Orthodox Economists*. Oxford: Blackwell, 1973.

Adam Smith   *Essays: Philosophical and Literary*. London: Ward, Lock and Co., no date.

Ron Stanfield   *The Economic Surplus and Neo-Marxism*. Lexington, Massachusetts: Lexington Books, 1973.

| Gordon Strong | *Adam Smith and the Eighteenth Century Concept of Social Progress.* St. Louis, Mo.: Eden Publishing House, 1932. |
| Paul Walston and Andrew Gamlele | *From Alienation to Surplus Value.* London: Sheed and Ward, 1972. |

THE 19TH CENTURY

John Chamberlain	*The Roots of Capitalism.* Princcton, New Jersey: Van Nostrand, 1959.
Louis Hacker	*The Triumph of American Capitalism: The Development of Forces in American History to the End of the Nineteenth Century.* New York: Simon and Schuster, 1940.
Leo Hausleiter	*The Machine Unchained: Revolution in the World Economic System from the First Steam Engine to the Crisis of Plenty.* London: Routledge, 1933.
Friedrich August von Hayek	*Capitalism and the Historians.* Chicago: University of Chicago Press, 1954.
John Hobson	*The Evolution of Modern Capitalism: A Study of Machine Production.* London: Allen and Uwin, 1949.
David S. Landes	*The Rise of Capitalism.* New York: MacMillan, 1966.
John Lord	*Capital and Steam Power: 1750-1800.* London: Cass, 1946.
Frederick Nussbaum	*A History of the Economic Institutions of Modern Europe.* New York: F. S. Crafts and Co., 1933.
Henri See	*Modern Capitalism: Its Origin and Evolution.* New York: N. Douglas, 1928.

CAPITALISM TODAY

| D. M. Gordon | Recession in Capitalism as Usual. *New York Times Magazine*, April 27, 1975, pp. 18-19 +. |

D. C. Harvey	Strengths of the Free Enterprise System. *Intellect*, 104, (January, 1976): 281-282.
L. H. Lapham	Capitalist Paradox. *Harper's*, 254, (March, 1977): 31-34 + .
Nation	Culture of Capitalism. April 19, 1975, p. 453-454.
A. Wolfe	Giving Up on Democracy: Capitalism Shows its Face. *Nation*, November 29, 1975, pp. 557-563.

Michael Barratt-Brown	*The Economics of Imperialism*. Harmondsworth: Penguin Education, 1974.
John Blair	*Seeds of Destruction: A Study in the Functional Weakness of Capitalism*. New York: Covici Friede, 1938.
John Brill	*Anti-Utopia: A Refutation of the Marxian Doctrine and a Defense of Capitalism*. Columbia, Missouri: Lucas Brothers, 1940.
Herman Cahn	*The Collapse of Capitalism*. Chicago: C. H. Kerr and Co., 1918.
James Cromwell and H. E. Czerivonky	*In Defence of Capitalism*. New York: C. Scribner's Sons, 1937.
Ambrose Hoskins	*The Mind of a Diehard: A Defence of the Social System*. London: The Labour Publishing Co. Ltd., 1925.
Michael Ivens	*The Case for Capitalism*. London: published in association with Aims of Industry by Michael Joseph, 1967.
Maurice Parmeliee	*Farewell to Poverty*. New York: J. Wiley and Sons Inc., 1935.
Frank Pease	*Pole to Panama: An Appeal for American Imperialism and a Defence of American Capitalism*. New York: R. Spelles, Inc., 1935.

FUTURE OF CAPITALISM

F. Byrom   Going Down the Drain. *Intellect*, 105, (January, 1977): 210.

R. L. Heilbroner   What Future for Capitalism? *Current*, 147, (January, 1973): 51-58.

R. L. Lesher   Can Capitalism Survive? The Unbelievable Growth of Government Power and Spending. *Vital Speeches*, September 15, 1975, pp. 731-734.

D. P. Moynihan   Capitalism's World Struggle for Survival. *Nation's Business*, 64, (February, 1976): 420-423.

B. A. Rogge   Will Capitalism Survive? *Vital Speeches*, July 1, 1974, pp. 564-568.

P. A. Samuelson   Capitalism in Twilight? *Newsweek*, July 7, 1976, p. 76.

J. Schneppwe   Can Capitalism Survive Rising Inflation? *Intellect*, 103, (November, 1974): 114-115.

A. Smith   Last Days of Cowboy Capitalism. *Atlantic Monthly*, 230, (September, 1972): 43.55.

H. C. Wallich   Future of Capitalism. *Newsweek*, January 22, 1973, p. 62.

Albert Baster   *The Twilight of American Capitalism: An Economic Interpretation of the New Deal*. London: P. S. King and Son Ltd., 1937.

Lawrence Dennis   *Is Capitalism Doomed?* New York: Harper and Brothers, 1932.

Scott Nearing   *The Twilight of Empire: An Economic Interpretation of Imperialist Cycles*. New York: Vanguard Press, 1930.

Therman Arnold   *The Future of Democratic Capitalism*. Philadelphia: (and others)   University of Pennsylvania Press, 1950.

The Editor

BRUNO LEONE received his B.A. (Phi Kappa Phi) from Arizona State University and his M.A. in history from the University of Minnesota. A Woodrow Wilson Fellow (1967), he is currently an instructor at Metropolitan Community College, Minneapolis, where he has taught history, anthropology, and political science. In 1974-75, he was awarded a Fellowship by the National Endowment for the Humanities to research the intellectual origins of American Democracy.

SERIES EDITORS

GARY E. McCUEN received his A.B. degree in history from Ripon College. He also has an M.S.T. degree in history from Wisconsin State University in Eau Claire, Wisconsin. He has taught social studies at the high school level and is co-origina-tor of the *Opposing Viewpoints Series*, *Future Planning Game Series*, *Photo Study Cards* and *Opposing Viewpoints Cassettes*. He is currently working on new materials to be published by Greenhaven Press.

DAVID L. BENDER is a history graduate from the University of Minnesota. He also has an M.A. in government from St. Mary's University in San Antonio, Texas. He has taught social problems at the high school level and is a co-originator of the *Opposing Viewpoints Series*, *Future Planning Game Series*, *Photo Study Cards* and *Opposing Viewpoints Cassettes*. He is currently working on new materials that will be published by Greenhaven Press.